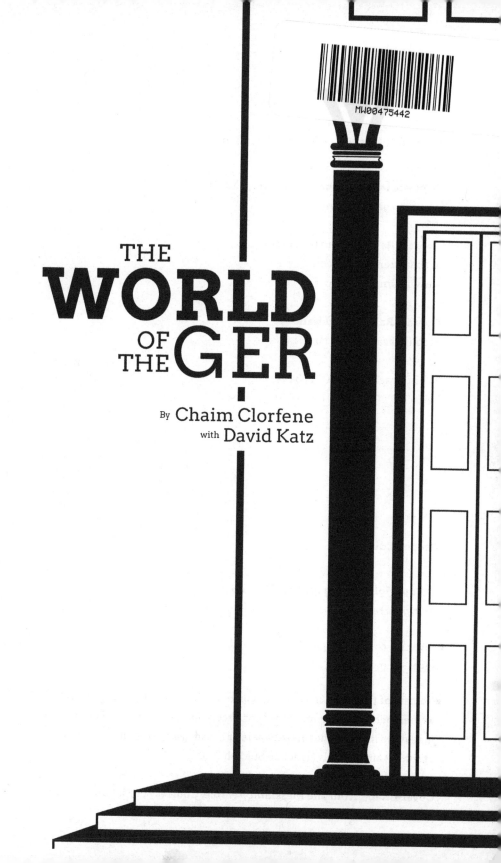

THE
WORLD
OF
THE GER

By Chaim Clorfene
with David Katz

Other Books by the Author

Confessions of a Jewish Cultbuster

The Path of the Righteous Gentile

Mikdash d'Meshicha (The Messianic Temple)

To purchase copies of *The World of the Ger*

visit www.gergear.com

Contact Rabbi Chaim Clorfene

at shaarster@gmail.com

www.chaimclorfene.com

Contact Rabbi David Katz

at soulmazal@gmail.com

Tel. in Israel 972 (0)50 577 3444

Tel in U.S. 702 577 1891

Second Edition

Cover image: from *The Messianic Temple*, Courtesy of Menorah Books.

Acknowledgements

With heartfelt gratitude to *Hashem Yisborach*, our Savior and our Redeemer, Whose guidance and blessings were constant throughout this great project. And thanks to Rabbi David Pesach Katz; his courage and brilliant scholarship produced fruit from the Tree of Life that permeates every word of this book.

Special thanks goes to Susan Strickland who somehow knew this was going to be a book before we did and helped make it happen.

And we are grateful to all our friends and associates who also helped make this project a realty – Ruven (Walter) Schwartz, Ariela Clorfene, Miriam Katz for believing in the Soul Mazal vision and seeing it through to success, Danny and Gila Brock, Ron Van Arsdale, Dr. Juan Mayorga, April Janutka for her creativity and generous contribution of time and effort, Russell and Teresa Kirk, Chad Russell, Lillian Berman Goldfarb, Tamar Yonah, the greater Soul Mazal team and family whose contributors are too numerous to name, Ross Bearden, Ken Jeffries, Jason Specht, Joe Indeminico, Rod Bryant and Ira Michaelson and their Light to the Nations work, Denise and Roy Raterta and the many Gerim they have made in the Philippines, Amnon Goldberg, and the rabbis who advised us along the way: Rabbi Yerachmiel Silver, z'l, Rabbi Mattityahu Glazerson, Rabbi Yosef Trachtman, Rabbi Raphael Weingot and the Shalom Rav family, and for the trust of the dozens of people who pre-ordered the book and showed great patience.

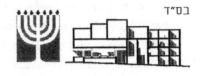

ישיבת דבר ירושלים

האקדמיה הירושלמית ללמודי יהדות (ע"ר)

YESHIVAT DVAR YERUSHALAYIM

The Jerusalem Academy of Jewish Studies

ראש הישיבה : הרב ברוך הורוויץ

3rd of Tamuz, 5774

July 1, 2014

Harav Hagaon Chaim Clorfene, author of the book *The Path of the Righteous Gentile*, and Rav David Pesach Katz, have written the important book, *The World of the Ger (Mankind)*, where they make clear the goal of the righteous Gentiles of the nations, so they can be happy and fulfilled as the great and righteous people that they are. This book will strengthen their identity and they will recognize what is important for them, especially now since we are so close to the fulfillment of the prophecy of *Tzefaniah 3:9, "I will change the people to a pure language that they may all call upon the name of the L-rd."*

With full blessing,

Harav Yoel Schwartz

שְׁמַע יִשְׂרָאֵל, יְיָ אֱלֹהֵינוּ, יְיָ | אֶחָד:

Hear O Israel, the Lord is our God, the Lord is One.

— Deuteronomy 6:4

"The Lord Who is our God now, but not the God of the other nations, will be one Lord in the future, as it says in Zephaniah 3:9, 'For then I will bestow pure speech upon the peoples so that they may all call upon the Name of the Lord;' and it says in Zechariah 14:9, 'In that day the Lord shall be One and His Name One.'"

– Commentary of Rashi (Rabbi Shlomo ben Yitzhak 1040-1105)

Jewish law (halacha) has never addressed this 'Gentile of the future' because it is not the way of the rabbis to make rulings about a *"davar shelo ba l'olam,"* a thing that has not yet come into the world. But today, this evolved Gentile exists, perhaps for the first time ever, but certainly for the first time since the destruction of Solomon's Temple more than 2500 years ago. *The World of the Ger* is about this Gentile.

The World of the Ger
is dedicated to the blessed memory of
the man who started it all,

Dr. Vendyl Jones, zy"a

25 Sivan 5690 – 27 Teves 5771
May 29, 1930 – December 27, 2010

In 1967, prior to the Six Day War, Dr. Vendyl Jones tried to enlist in the Israeli Defense Forces, but was turned down because they did not want to put an American civilian in harm's way. Then, when the war began, Vendyl was making his way on foot towards Jerusalem when he came upon an IDF trench near Radar Hill. Once more, he offered himself as a soldier. The commander refused to give him a gun and instead handed him a pair binoculars and told to keep an eye towards the road to Tel Aviv. It was at this observation post that Dr. Jones spotted sixty-six Jordanian anti-tank positions and four Jordanian personnel bunkers in the valley below, and was credited as having been a significant factor in Israel's defeat of the Jordanians. Later that day, he hitched a ride to Jerusalem and arrived near the Temple Mount just in time to hear the blast of a shofar coming from the vicinity of the *Kotel* (Western Wall). He said that the sound was etched in his soul forever.

And Moses said to Jethro, his father-in-law:
"Please do not leave us, for you know our encampments in the wilderness, and you shall be as eyes for us (Numbers 10:31)."

Susan Strickland

May *Hashem* open the hearts, minds and eyes of the *Gerim* as they embark on this wonderful journey into *Hashem's* place for them in the world. Through the World of the *Ger* you will be blessed with endless revelations that will make your heart sing. May this book bring eternal clarity to all who read and share it with others.

The Netiv Center, Humble Texas

The Netiv Center for Torah study is an unaffiliated, Orthodox outreach center, geared toward the non-Jewish community. Providing weekly Torah studies and a free research library, Netiv has become a vibrant Noahide/Ger community center. With the ever-growing need for scholarly research on the subject, Rabbis David Katz and Chaim Clorfene bring new insight and illumination to "The World of the Ger". Our community is grateful to Rabbi Clorfene for taking the time to write this inspiring and informative book. "World of the Ger" is a literary wellspring of information for anyone wanting to connect to God through Judaism. What seems like a tidal wave of people from the nations are leaving their various forms of idolatry in order to take on the yoke of HaShem. In this book, those people have a much needed addition to the scarce resources that help guide their way. Netiv dedicates this book to the seeking soul.

NETIV
www.netiv.net

שלמה בן גבריאל הכהן

Steve HaKohen Kaplan

and

רון בן גבריאל הכהן

Ronnie HaKohen Kaplan

in loving memory of their parents

שרה בת ר׳ אליה דוד

Selma Kaplan, *aleh hashalom*
April 27, 1928-November 13, 1980
"forever in our hearts"

גבריאל ב״ר שלמה הכהן

George HaKohen Kaplan, *alav hashalom*
April 8, 1924 - January 20, 1998
"To know him was to love him"

May their souls be bound up in the bond of life
with the souls of the righteous in Gan Eden.

Joseph and April Janutka

With gratitude to *Hashem*, we lovingly dedicate this first edition to our children, and to all of *Am Yisrael* with whose lives theirs may intersect:

Myles, Seth, Madelyn, Isaac, Leah

May you be blessed to find within these pages the answers and guidance upon which our own path was founded. And in honor of the *Yehudim* who *Hashem* placed in our lives, to be His Light to the Nations, we gratefully thank:

Rabbi Chaim Clorfene
Sam (Shmuel) Peak
Rabbi Chaim and Rena Richman
Rabbi David Katz

Chaim Noach HaLevi Clorfene
and **Ariela Yehudis Clorfene**

In memory of their beloved parents

ישראל בער בן מנשה מניא
שרה פייגא בת זאב יהושע

Judge Irwin HaLevi Clorfene, *alav hashalom*
and **Sara Brin Clorfene**, *aleh hashalom*

*"May their souls be bound up in the bond of life with
the souls of the righteous in Gan Eden."*

✡ ✡ ✡ ✡

Ze'ev ben Ephraim HaLevi Kamen
and his daughter **Liba Gittel** *bas* **Naomi**

in memory of his beloved parents

Ephraim HaLevi
ben **Raphael Kamen**, *alav hashalom*

and

Chaya Faigela Kamen
bas **Yitzhak Yakov**, *aleh hashalom*

*"May their souls be bound up in the bond of life
with the souls of the righteous in Gan Eden."*

Gloria Culver

In memory of my late husband,

John Culver

who dearly loved Vendyl Jones, of blessed memory,
and delighted in being his Torah student.

✡ ✡ ✡ ✡

Russell and Teresa Kirk

"Satan has no power over two nations who are together."
(Babylonian Talmud, Shabbat 32a)

Ben and Nadeen Katz
"A little bit of light dispels much darkness"

✡ ✡ ✡ ✡

Jason Specht
In dedication to the most important man that I have ever met.
The man who gave me my soul. My hero, my mentor, my friend **Sam Peak.**

✡ ✡ ✡ ✡

Noahide Canada
"Blessed is the Lord of the universe, from Whose bounty the heritage and spiritual identity of B'nai Noah is revealed in our time." Noahide Canada also wants to give many thanks to Rabbi Clorfene and Rabbi Katz for their great work.

✡ ✡ ✡ ✡

Deana McGlauflin
Lewis Waldfogel (1897-1979)
Planted the Jewish seed and Vendyl helped it grow.

✡ ✡ ✡ ✡

Karen and Tom Maitlen
To our beloved friend and teacher Vendyl Jones, of blessed memory.
Thank you for putting us on the path of Torah.

✡ ✡ ✡ ✡

Ed Stribling
In blessed memory of Vendyl Jones who was instrumental in helping me discover the fact that I am a Noahide by answering my questions and teaching me Torah.

Vendyl Jones, Jr.

I am so grateful for all the knowledge my father had shared with
me over the years. If it weren't for him, I do not know what
I would have believed today.
What I am and what I believe has made me solid as a rock.

✡ ✡ ✡ ✡

Glenn and Michelle Magnusson

With much love and gratitude to all our teachers of Torah.
May the Light of Torah continue to be spread among the nations.

✡ ✡ ✡ ✡

Sonia and Rodolfo Garza

With gratitude and love for Vendyl Jones, of blessed memory

✡ ✡ ✡ ✡

Bob Wells

In honor and appreciation of the Bais Menachem community
Chicago.

✡ ✡ ✡ ✡

Jason LaCross

To our children **Calob, Cullen, Austin, Aaron, and Katelyn**
May *HaShem* show you His ways, and guide you in His truth
and teach you.

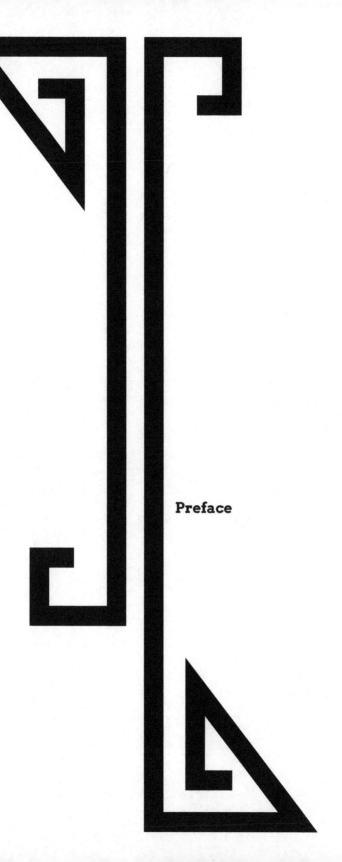

Preface

A new light came down in the 1960's. People were put in motion physically and spiritually. The global village was beginning to look with a jaundiced eye at gross materialism. There was talk about liberation and enlightenment. The youth were being led towards the light by poets and minstrels:

> How does it feel,
> To be on your own,
> With no direction home,
> Like a complete unknown,
> Like a rolling stone.

Bob Dylan and Donovan and dozens of other social revolutionaries were using music and code to stir the hearts of the masses and get them to get up and march. They did not exactly know where they were headed, but they were certain it was going to be better than what their parents, teachers, churches, and governments had given them. And then, the Beatles surprised everyone by entering the spiritual realm. They went to India, met a guru, and brought a few million of their followers to Hinduism. That was a costly mistake. Hinduism had too many gods to count when you're stoned.

In their desire to reject middle class values, many of the youth of the sixties, lacking wisdom and understanding, embraced pagan idolatry. And everything crashed. The sixties became a "was" and a "what might have been." All of this was in the realm of spiritual impurity, what the Kabbalists call the *sitra achara*, the "other side."

In the realm of *kedusha* (holiness), a new chapter of an ancient story was being written. In 1967, the same year that the Beatles released Sergeant Pepper's Lonely Hearts Club and The Magical Mystery Tour, Egypt, Syria, and Jordan, were mobilizing to attack Israel from three sides and drive the Jews into the Mediterranean.

Then, on June 5, 1967, Israel launched a surprise strike against Egyptian airfields, and in six days, Israel shattered the military forces of all three Arab states. Millions of people around the world recognized the hand of God in this. It was an open miracle. The Pillar of Cloud was not there, but everybody saw it in their mind's eye. The hearts of the righteous swelled with pride and excitement as they recalled the words of Exodus, *"And the*

Egyptians said, 'Let us flee from before Israel, for the Lord is fighting for them against Egypt (Exodus 14:25).'"

On June 7, two days into the war, Israeli paratroopers fought their way past bullet-riddled Zion Gate, through the Old City of Jerusalem, and took back the Western Wall and the Temple Mount, bringing the holiest site on earth under Jewish control for the first time in 2000 years.

And then, lo and behold, Israel shocked the world by handing custody of the Temple Mount back to the Arabs. It was no secret that this action was taken to block Jewish plans to rebuild the Temple. But the truth is that returning the Temple Mount to the Arabs was God's decision. The land of Israel may be conquered through war. Even Jerusalem may be taken by force. But the Temple Mount can be acquired only by peace, as the Lord instructed Zerubbabel, the builder of the Second Temple (Zechariah 4:6), *"Not by military force and not by physical strength but by My spirit, says the Lord of Hosts."*

The Lubavitcher Rebbe, *zy'a*, called the Six Day War the Great Shofar, as it says in the *Amidah*, the central Jewish prayer, *"Sound the Great Shofar for our freedom, raise the banner to gather our exiles and speedily gather us together from the four corners of the earth to our land."*

Rabbi Abraham Isaac HaKohen Kook, the first chief rabbi of Israel, taught that the Great Shofar is an awakening of spiritual greatness and idealism.

By Divine Providence, the awakening happened in a most unexpected place – deep in the heart of Texas. In that year, 1967, Dr. Vendyl Jones formed the Judaic-Christian Research Institute, for the study and dissemination of the Seven Laws of the Children of Noah, the moral code given by God to Noah after the Flood. It is also known as Universal Torah.

Dr. Jones, an ex-Baptist minister, was a world class archaeologist, having made important Biblical archaeological discoveries. He deciphered the Copper Scroll (one of the Dead Sea Scrolls) and this led him to the discovery of nearly 900 pounds of the Holy Temple incense (*ketoret*) and the afarsimon anointing oil. But Dr. Jones' greatest discovery was himself. He discovered that he was a Ben Noah, a Noahide, a species of *homo sapiens* that had been extinct for 2500 years.

In the times of King David and King Solomon, the land of Israel's population included hundreds of thousands of righteous Gentiles. This is the *Ger Toshav*, the foreign resident mentioned in the Torah. And so it was throughout the First Temple period. But then, the Kingdom of Israel was exiled to Assyria as the Ten Lost Tribes. And the Kingdom of Judea was exiled to Babylon (those few who Nebuchadnezzar left alive). And the Noahide (all *Gerim Toshavim* are Noahides) got lost in the shuffle.

From those days till today, there have been few mentions of the Noahide in Jewish history, certainly nothing the magnitude of what Dr. Vendyl Jones began in 1967.

Dr. Jones' work on behalf of the Seven Noahide Laws has flourished. He lived to see the Noahide Movement grow from a handful of friends and neighbors to thousands of Noahides in the Americas, throughout Europe, in India, Australia and cities throughout the world. And the movement is blossoming quickly, just like Aaron's rod. And this is what the Talmud (*Baba Batra, 35b*) means by, "*A Noahide who learns Torah is equal to the Kohen Gadol (High Priest)*." It tells him that his staff will bloom with buds and almonds quickly and simultaneously, because he has been chosen for great things by *Hashem*, the God of Israel. With this sentiment, we dedicate this book, *The World of the Ger*, to the memory of Dr. Vendyl Jones, zy'a, the man who started it all.

Rabbi Chaim Noach HaLevi Clorfene
Tzfat, Israel
12 Tamuz 5774
July 9, 2014

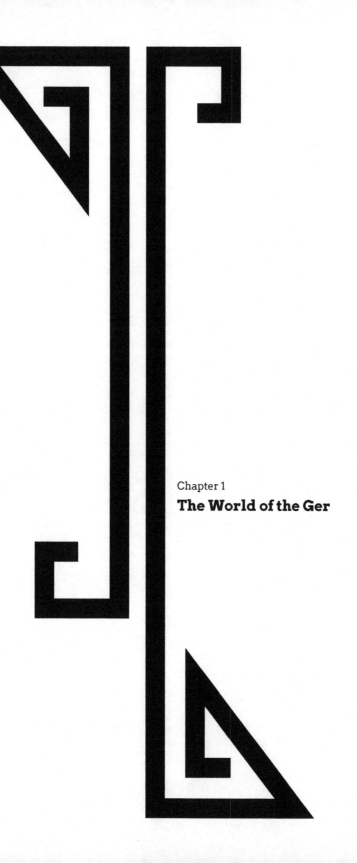

Chapter 1
The World of the Ger

The World of the Ger represents a departure from the usual Noahide literature[1] in that it consists primarily of *Aggadot*. These are the parables, stories and historical narratives that form the character and world view of a people. With Hashem's help, these holy Jewish teachings will lead to a strengthening of the cultural and spiritual identity of *B'nai Noah*, the Children of Noah.

This is probably as good a time and place as any to address the nagging problem of confused and troublesome nomenclature. What do we call the Children of Noah? What do they call themselves? The default term that everybody uses and nobody seems to like is "Noahide."

Noahide is derivative of *B'nai Noah* in the same manner that Israelite is derivative of *B'nai Yisrael*. But if Noahide is like Israelite, then why is it Noahide instead of Noahite? Because it is wrong! Noahide is an adjective being used as a noun. Noahite is actually correct. Nevertheless, the term Noahide seems to get the job done simply, so Noahide is used and understood and accepted everywhere.

But for those who know and care, there is a more correct term. The problem is that it does *not* get the job done simply. In fact, it is extremely complicated and has already been the cause of far too many debates and arguments. It is the term that the Torah itself uses for the *B'nai Noah*. The term is *Ger*. The plural is *Gerim*.

If you look up the word *Ger* in any Hebrew-English dictionary you will find an assortment of words such as: stranger, foreigner, alien, outsider, and proselyte.

Ask an Orthodox Jew what a *Ger* is, and he will tell you that a *Ger* is a Gentile who has converted to become a Jew.

The Torah agrees with this, but considers it only half the story. The Torah adds a factor that few people appreciate: a *Ger* can also be a Noahide who has come from afar to be close to the Jewish people in the land of Israel or even outside the land of Israel. He has come close to the Jews because,

---

1. A Noahide is a Gentile who observes the Universal Torah, that is, the seven commandments given by God to Noah on behalf of all mankind.

in the venerable words of Vendyl Jones[2], "I love the holy trinity – God, the Torah, and the Jewish people."

So it turns out that there are two types of *Gerim*, the *Ger Toshav*, who is a foreign resident, a *Noahide*, and the *Ger Tzedek*, the righteous proselyte, who has become a Jew through conversion. There are sixty verses in the Torah that mention the *Ger* and each verse must be carefully studied to determine which *Ger* is meant. Sometimes a verse will refer only to the *Ger Toshav*. Sometimes it will refer only to the *Ger Tzedek*. And most often, in the vast majority of cases, the verse is talking about both the *Ger Toshav* and the *Ger Tzedek*, all with a single mention of word *Ger*[3].

According to *halacha* (Jewish Law), a *Ger Toshav* is theoretically required to come before a court of three Rabbis and declare his intention to observe the Seven Laws of the Children of Noah[4]. Then he is accepted as a *Ger Toshav* and is officially settled in the land of Israel and is entitled to support from the Jewish community.

These *Gerim* are a people, as distinct as any other on earth, except that their existence is defined exclusively by their relationship to the God of Israel, the Torah, and the Jewish people.

The truth is that before there was a Jew there was a *Ger*. Abraham said to the men of Heth (Genesis 23:4), *"I am a Ger and a Toshav with you."*

Four hundred years later, Moses said (Exodus 2:22), *"I was a Ger in a foreign land."*

And four hundred years after that, King David wrote (Psalms 39:13), *"I am a Ger with You, a Toshav as were all my fathers."*

---

2. Vendyl Jones (1930-2010) was a ex-Baptist minister turned Noahide, a world class archaeologist and a dynamic leader of the Noahide movement.

3. Actually, the term *Ger Tzedek* is rabbinic and it is never mentioned in the Torah itself. And in the period of the Talmud and early rabbinic commentaries, *Ger Tzedek* is sometimes applied to a *Ger Toshav* who is on a high spiritual level. We warned you that this was not simple.

4. See page 10 and the view of Rogatchover Gaon.

Abraham the Noahide

Abraham called himself a *Ger* because he was a Hebrew living among Canaanites, a foreign resident. Abraham is the father of all *Gerim*, both Jewish converts and Noahide *Gerim*. Even though he is called the first Jew, Abraham was a Noahide and not a Jew at all. Technically, the Jewish people were born at Mount Sinai when they heard the voice of God say the Ten Commandments and were given the 613 *mitzvot* of the Torah. Abraham was commanded only in the Seven Laws of Noah and the *mitzvah* of circumcision.

However, Abraham is called the first Jew because he began the rectification of the sin of Adam which was completed at Mount Sinai. And even though Abraham and Sara were not commanded to observe the Shabbat and the entire Torah, they did so voluntarily, having received this knowledge as a sacred oral tradition from Shem the son of Noah[5].

Moses the Noahide.

Everything the Jewish people know about conversion, they learned from the Exodus from Egypt. During that miraculous event, Israelite men were circumcised and immersed in a *mikvah*[6]. Israelite women also immersed in a *mikvah*. And both men and women accepted upon themselves the Torah as a doctrine of life, as King Solomon wrote[7], *"It is a Tree of Life for those who grasp it."* The people at Sinai said, *"Na'aseh v'nishmah – we will do and then we will hear,"* accepting the commandments unhesitatingly, unquestioningly, lovingly, because it came from the God of Abraham, Isaac, and Jacob, even before they knew what the commandments were. There is nothing that can diminish that merit, not now or ever.

---

5. Genesis Rabba 43:6.

6. A ritual pool of living waters. Immersion in a *mikvah* removes spiritual impurity of a person or object.

7. Proverbs 3:18.

When Moses said he was a *Ger* in a strange land, he meant that he had been a Hebrew living in the land of Egypt. Like Abraham, Moses dwelled among people not his own. At Mount Sinai, Moses became a *Ger Tzedek*, a Jewish convert, along with everyone else. Bearing this in mind, it is a plain and obvious fact that God gave the entire Torah only to *Gerim* and their children. All Jews are the children of *Gerim*.

King David the Ger

David was neither a convert nor a Noahide. He was an *Ezrach*, a native born Jew. His father was Jesse and his mother was Nitzevet, a nice Jewish lady[8]. So why did David call himself a *Ger*? It is possible to say that he was referring to his great-grandmother, Ruth, who came from Moabite stock. Or, that he was treated as an outsider by his father and seven brothers. Or, that he lived like a *Ger* among Philistines in Kiryat Gat when he fled from King Saul.

But there is a more abstract reason that David considered himself a *Ger*. David was on an exalted spiritual and intellectual level, as it says (I Samuel 16:13), *"And Samuel took the horn of oil and anointed him in the midst of his brothers; and a Spirit of the Lord passed over David from that day on."*

David knew what the *Ger* is in essence – the abstract *Ger* – and he felt he was that. David was saying that he is a *Ger* in this world, an alien just passing through. His true home is the God of Israel. God is the place of the world.

Jews and Gerim

One of the most salient aspects of being a *Ger*, either a Jewish convert or a Noahide, is the relationship with the Jewish people. The Jew and the *Ger* are inextricably bound together. It can be wonderful or horrible or both. Either way, the dynamic between Jew and *Ger* is vital. Without the Jew as a light to the nations, the *Ger* would grope in darkness forever. And

---

8. Babylonian Talmud, 91a. David's mother's name is mentioned nowhere in Scripture, but was known from the oral tradition and is recorded in the Talmud.

without the *Ger*, the Jew might never reach *Geulah Sheleimah*, the Final Redemption.

This *Jew-Ger* relationship is comparable to newlyweds and their in-laws. How does the new husband relate to his wife's parents? And how does the new wife get along with her husband's parents? It can be pure love and joy, each one instantly accepted into the new family like a son or a daughter. Or, it can be stiff and formal, distant, distrusting and uncomfortable. Or, it can be bad chemistry altogether with everyone despising each other, God forbid.

Generally, but not always, these relationships improve with age as time softens feelings of otherness. So it is with the Jew and the *Ger*. As time passes, Jews and *Gerim*, living side by side on the land, learn to grow into one community, as it says (Leviticus 19:34), *"The Ger who dwells with you shall be unto you as the native-born among you, and you shall love him like yourself, because you were Gerim in the land of Egypt: I am the Lord your God."*

The verse tells the Jewish people that they must love the *Ger* as they love themselves. The question is: Which *Ger* is the verse talking about, the Jewish convert or the Noahide or both?

The verse says that the Jew should love the *Ger* *"because you were Gerim in Egypt."* Were the Israelites converts in Egypt? No, they were foreign residents, Hebrews living among Egyptians. Therefore, the *Ger* of this verse must include the *Ger Toshav*, a Noahide living among Israelites. It also must include the *Ger Tzedek*, the Jewish convert, because it simply fits.

In truth, a Jewish convert should not be called a Ger, or the feminine *Gioret*, except when the need arises to identify his or her roots, such as when an offer of marriage is proposed. The Talmud says[9], *"When the convert emerges from the mikvah, he is an Israelite in every way."* If he is an Israelite in every way, why are you calling him a stranger, a Ger? In fact, if the feelings of a Jewish convert are hurt by being called a Ger, then to call him that may be a transgression of, *"Do not taunt or oppress the Ger (Exodus 22:20)."*

According to tradition, the *Ger Toshav's* official status is dependent on the Jubilee Year, which is the year after the seventh Sabbatical Year in a

---

9. Babylonian Talmud, Yebamot 47a.

fifty year cycle[10]. At the beginning of the Jubilee Year, liberty is proclaimed throughout the land of Israel. Property that was sold during the previous forty-nine years returns to the original tribal and family holdings and Hebrew slaves are freed.

Without a Jubilee Year, rabbinic courts do not officially accept *Gerim Toshavim*. And there has not been a Jubilee Year since the destruction of the First Temple more than 2500 years ago. This is precisely the reason why the *Noahide Ger* is unknown, confusing and even upsetting to many religious Jewish people. The *Noahide Ger* seems to have popped up out of nowhere to do little more than challenge the religious Jew's thinking. For no matter what you tell a religious Jew about the *Noahide Ger*, he will answer you with, *"That's not what I was told!"*

There has been no Jubilee Year since the days of the Prophet Ezekiel because it requires the majority of the Jewish people to live in the land of Israel. And ever since the First Temple was destroyed, there has never been a clear majority of the Jewish people living in the Land.

While on the subject of Jubilee Year, we should note that it was on *Rosh Hashana* of the very last Jubilee Year[11] that the Prophet Ezekiel saw a vision of the third Temple that would one day complete the Final Redemption, as it says (Ezekiel 37:28), *"And the nations will know that I am the Lord Who sanctifies Israel when My Sanctuary is in their midst forever."* This is bound up with the soul of the *Noahide Ger*. He has every right to mourn for the loss of the Holy Temple, but rather than mourn for the destruction of the Second Temple, he mourns because we have not yet built the Third Temple.

The rationale for requiring the Jubilee Year in order to accept the *Ger Toshav* is somewhat intricate, but here it is in a nutshell: The Torah allows a *Ger Toshav* to sell himself as a slave if he is destitute, but he must go free in the Jubilee Year. If there is no Jubilee Year, there is no legal mechanism

---

10. Leviticus 25:10

11. The Hebrew year 3352 (572 B.C.E.)

to free him. Therefore, the Rabbis will not officially accept the *Ger Toshav* until there is a Jubilee Year.[12]

Had the matter of accepting the *Ger Toshav* been decided by reason rather than tradition, the ruling could have been somewhat different. The Rabbis could have said: *"We accept Gerim Toshavim today, but they are forbidden to sell themselves into slavery until the Jubilee Year returns."* But that is not the way it went.

At first glance, it might appear that the Rabbis have closed the door on the *Ger Toshav*, at least for the present. But the opposite is true. Because the rabbinic courts are powerless to accept the *Ger Toshav* due to a snag in the *halacha*, the Rogatchover Gaon[13] ruled that a Noahide can become a *Ger Toshav* on his own by simply accepting the Seven Laws of Noah, without any need for rabbinic approval[14]. And even on this basis, the Jewish community is obliged to support him if he falls on hard times, and he may take a share of the agricultural gifts for the poor[15]. And he is permitted to observe any or all the *mitzvot* of the Torah, including Shabbat and Talmud Torah, just like his father Abraham, the first *Ger Toshav*. According to the

---

12. For the Jubilee Year to be functional, the majority of Jews have to live in Israel. This has not happened since the destruction of Solomon's Temple in the year 3338 (586 B.C.E.). There was no Jubilee Year in the Second Temple period or ever since.

13. Rabbi Josef Rosen (1856-1936), one of the most prominent Talmudic scholars of the 20th century. He gave rabbinic ordination (smicha) to Rabbi Menachem M. Schneerson, the Lubavitcher Rebbe.

14. *Razin D'Orayta*, p. 97, section 33, *Ger Toshav in the time of the Temple and now*.

15. Torah ordained agricultural gifts to the poor: the corner of the field, forgotten sheaves, fallen grain in the field and fallen grapes and small bunches of grapes left on the vine. See Leviticus 19:9, 10.

Vilna Gaon, if the *Ger Toshav* is living on the land, he obligated in all 613 *mitzvot*, including *brit milah* (ritual circumcision)[16].

Settling the Ger Toshav on the land[17].

> #### Excerpt from Gerim 3:4:[18]
> We do not settle him [the *Ger Toshav*] on the frontier or in an unhealthy district, but in a pleasant district in the Land of Israel where he can find opportunity for his occupation, as it is stated (Deuteronomy 23:17), "He shall dwell with you, in the midst of you, in the place which he shall choose within one of your gates where it pleases him most; you shall not wrong him."

on the frontier: The reason that the *Ger Toshav* is not settled near the borders of Israel is twofold: a) He would be vulnerable to attack by foreign neighbors who resent his connection to the Jewish people. b) He would be befriended by foreign neighbors who would try to lure him to their heathen ways.

We have a rare situation at this point in history. Not since the end of the First Temple period,[19] has there been such a great wave of Noahides who identify themselves as *Gerim*. And it would seem that a new era of interpersonal relationships between Torah observant Jews and *Noahide Gerim* has begun.

---

16. *Aderet Eliyahu, Haazinu 32:9.* Rabbi Eliyahu of Vilna (1720-1797), one of the great Talmudist and Kabbalists of the 18th century, and the leader of Lithuanian Jewry.

17. This will not happen until the Jubilee Year and *batei din* accept *Gerim Toshavim* officially. However, the *Ger Toshav* of today may live on the land of Israel on his own.

18. One of the minor Talmudic tractates found at the end of *Seder Nezikin* in many editions of the Babylonian Talmud.

19. The Hebrew years 2928-3338 (996 BCE - 586 BCE). This was the Temple that King Solomon built and the Babylonian King Nebuchadnezzar destroyed.

The Jewish people will be cautiously curious about the *Noahide Ger* entering their synagogues and their communities. But they will learn to accept him because he is mentioned by name in the Ten Commandments and because he proclaims as his faith: *Hear O Israel, the Lord our God, the Lord is One.*[20]

The Jewish people have been given the responsibility of sustaining the *Ger Toshav* who lives among them.

> ### Deuteronomy 14:21:
> *You shall not eat any nevelah; you shall give it to the Ger within your gates that he may eat it; or you may sell it to the Nochri.*

nevelah: an animal that died in any manner other than ritual Jewish slaughter (*shechita*).

to the Ger: This can only be referring to the *Ger Toshav* since a *Ger Tzedek* (Jewish convert) is forbidden to eat *nevelah*.

you shall give it: to the *Ger Toshav* as a gift without receiving payment.

Nochri: A visiting foreigner who has not embraced the Seven Laws of Noah.

you shall sell it: The *Nochri* is not a trusted neighbor. He does not receive free gifts of food because the Jewish people are not obliged to sustain him.

This verse is the scriptural source for the Jewish community's duty to sustain the *Ger Toshav*. The obligation extends beyond giving him meat for food; it includes all forms of sustenance, including spiritual. In this light, it is forbidden for a Jew to send the *Ger* back to the pit, his former idolatry.

---

20. Deuteronomy 6:4.

The Way of the Ger

Where does the Noahide begin his way as a *Ger*? The Talmud[21] tells us: *"In every generation a man should visualize himself as if he came out of Egypt."*

The *Noahide Ger* and *Gioret* need to see themselves as having just come out of Egypt. They begin their liberation and enlightenment and journey with God the same way the Israelites did more than 3300 years ago – with the Exodus. On the first night of the holiday of Passover, they eat *matzah* and *maror* (bitter herbs), drink four cups of wine, dip twice, lean and recite the *Haggadah*. Passover was, is, and always will be the beginning, because redemption begins with freedom.

From the Sulam's preface to the Zohar:[22]

To be worthy of redemption, one must be *pashut*[23] free of external connections. The purity of being pashut renders a person fit as an instrument of redemption.

It is generally known that when something is *pashut*, it is stripped of outside attachments, and stands independently. It follows then that the one who is singled out for redemption can have no connection to a master, for to be considered pashut, a person must not be subordinate to one who rules over him, for freedom and redemption are one thing, as it says (Exodus 20:2), *"I am the Lord your God, who took you out of the land of Egypt, out of the house of slavery."*

Therefore, it is as clear as day that when things are interconnected, they are subjugated to each other and no part is deemed free. This is the opposite of *matzah*, the unleavened bread that we eat on Passover, the holiday of our Freedom.

In and of itself, *matzah* is *pashut*, free from the addition of other elements. It contains nothing but flour and water, and is kneaded, rolled

---

21. Babylonian Talmud, Pesachim 10:5.

22. Preface to the Zohar, 2b, commentary of the Sulam, Rabbi Judah Ashlag, z"l.

23. The Hebrew word pashut means simple or straight.

out, and baked. Conversely, leavened bread, *i.e.*, *chametz*,[24] in addition to flour and water, is combined with *se'or*, leavening, which attaches itself to every grain of flour, causing the dough to rise. As a result, the grains are not free, but under the influence of leavening.

Similarly, when one is subjugated to a master, he has not attained freedom. And freedom is the ingredient through which Redemption (*Geulah*) was created.

The prerequisites for the *Ger* to maintain freedom are three:

1. The *Ger* must use wisdom to avoid the traps that may be spread for him and that he spreads for himself. Therefore, he must learn wisdom.

2. The *Ger* must have the courage to break every yoke other than God's. This begins with breaking the yoke of idolatry, but continues throughout life as a protection against trading in one trap for another.

3. The *Ger* must learn to trust his Teacher.

Rabbi Joseph Gikatilia,[25] *z"l*, taught that any person whose heart is given over to perfecting his character traits, who straightens his path and his deeds, and pursues humility to the ultimate so that when he is insulted he does not return the insult, and when he hears himself being shamed does not answer, immediately the *Shechina* rests upon him and he does not need to learn from a person of flesh and blood, for the Spirit of God (*Ruach Elokim*) teaches him.

---

24. It is forbidden to eat *chametz* on Passover (Exodus 12:15). *Chametz* is anything made from one of the five grains, wheat, rye, barley, oats, and spelt that has touched water and is allowed to ferment, which takes about 18 minutes.

25. Rabbi Joseph Gikatilia (1248-circa 1305), was a Spanish Kabbalist whose work, *Shaarei Orah*, was considered by the *Arizal* and the *Vilna Gaon* as the gateway to the Torah's mystical teachings.

Therefore, the Rambam taught[26] that in the Messianic Era, the occupation of the entire world will be solely to know God, as it says (Isaiah 11:9), *"The world will be filled with the knowledge of the Lord as water fills the sea."*

✡ ✡ ✡ ✡

A *Ger* who lives outside the land of Israel is half a *Ger*, for it takes the land of Israel to complete the soul of a *Ger*. But if one cannot live in the land, he can yearn for it, pray for it, learn to read and pronounce Biblical Hebrew, and make his world a little corner of Israel. If he does this, with *Hashem's* help, he will accomplish what he needs to accomplish. And he can rely on this, for Moses, a *Ger*, lived outside the land.

---

26. Mishneh Torah, Laws of Kings, 12:5

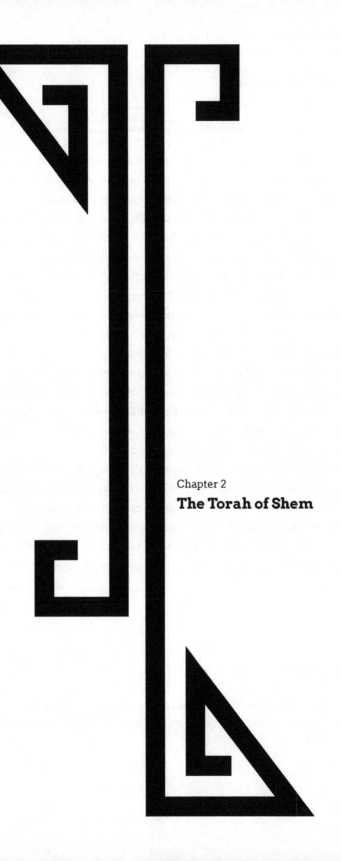

Chapter 2
The Torah of Shem

Part One: Primordial Torah.

God created the world and gave man the Torah so he would know how to live in it. Torah means instruction. It also means law, as in Deuteronomy 17:11, *"According to the law (Torah) which they shall teach you and according to the judgment which they shall tell you, you shall do."*

It is often said that the world was a moral and spiritual wasteland until Israel received the Torah on Mount Sinai.[1] Or, at least, until Abraham left his birthplace and came to the land that God showed him. But the truth is that the world was never a spiritual wasteland.[2] Torah has always been with man, right from the beginning. The primordial Torah is known as the Torah of Shem as we will learn, *b'ezrat Hashem*.

Adam received the Torah the same day he was created, as it says,[3] *"And the Lord God commanded the man, saying: 'Of every tree of the garden you may freely eat. But of the tree of the knowledge of good and evil you shall not eat from it, for in the day that you eat from it surely you shall die.'"* The Talmud[4] tells us that encoded within this single command are the Seven Universal Laws, which include prohibitions against idol worship, blasphemy, murder, theft, sexual perversion, eating the limb of a living animal, and failure to establish proper courts of law.

These laws were repeated to Noah after the Flood and became known as the *Seven Laws of the Children of Noah*. They were repeated again by Moses at Mount Sinai, where they became binding for all time, and where the Jewish people were instructed to teach them to the nations of the world.

The Noahide laws guarantee stability, continuity and permanence to any society that follows them. And they promise the individual a life

---

1. In the Hebrew year 2448 (1480 B.C.E.)

2. It is taught, however the first 2000 years were an epoch of *tohu* (chaos) because the *tikun* (rectification) of the sin of eating the forbidden fruit had not yet begun.

3. Genesis 2:16,17

4. Babylonian Talmud, Sanhedrin 56a.

blessed by God in this world and in the World to Come, as it says, *"It is a Tree of Life for those who grasp it."*[5]

These seven laws are the *nigleh* of the primordial Torah, the revealed teachings of God that have always been with mankind and are relevant to all people at all times.

There is another stream of Torah called *nistar*, the Torah's mystical or hidden teachings. Adam was given these teachings as well, but he received them only after he had been driven out of the Garden of Eden.

When Adam left the Garden of Eden and entered the outside world, he became a Ger by virtue of his living in a land not his own. His home was the Garden of Eden, but now he had to brave it in a strange new place. He had to face the unknown. This made him a Ger. The first man was the first Ger.

As a Ger, Adam could strive to return to the Garden of Eden or he could strive to transform the outside world into a new Garden of Eden and bring the creation to perfection. The Kabbalists say that it was God's plan to leave the world incomplete so that man, the crown of creation, could complete it.

God sent a scroll by the hand of the angel Raziel to Adam. The scroll is known as *Sefer Raziel*.[6] It was the first book. *Sefer Raziel* still exists, but people are warned not to learn it because it contains printers' errors and forgeries that have crept into the text over time. It also contains formulae for summoning and commanding angels, a practice which is strictly forbidden. Despite this, *Sefer Raziel* is considered a kosher holy book and many religious Jews keep a copy on their bookshelf in the belief that it brings special holiness to the home.

Unlike the laws of the Torah which are meant for everyone, the mystical teachings are given only to souls worthy of receiving them. People who shun the Kabbalah are in reality being shunned by the Kabbalah.

Sefer Raziel begins with Adam's prayer after he had been ejected from the Garden of Eden:

---

5. Proverbs 3:18.

6. Sefer is the word for book in Hebrew. Raziel means the secret of God.

The Prayer of Adam.

"Lord, God of the world, You created the whole world for glory, splendor, and power, and You made it according to Your will and Your kingship forever and ever, and for your glory for generation after generation. There is nothing concealed from You and nothing is hidden from Your eyes. You formed me by the work of Your hands and You gave me dominion over all Your creations that I should be master over what You made. But the crafty serpent aroused and seduced me with the tree of lust and desire. And also the wife of my bosom enticed me. And now, I do not know what will be and what will happen to my children, and what will happen to me and to the generations that will come after me.

"I know and understand that no living being can be considered righteous before you,[7] so what strength have I to face You? I have no mouth to answer for what I did and no eye to raise, for I sinned and was evil. And for my iniquity I was driven out till this day. I have ploughed and cultivated the earth to work for what I can take out of it, and now I am not as fearful or terrified about living on the earth as I was at first. For from the moment I ate from the Tree of Knowledge and transgressed Your word, my wisdom was taken from me and I am now ignorant, without knowledge and a fool. I do not understand what will be. Please now, merciful and gracious God, return Your great mercy to the crown of Your creation and upon the soul that You blew [into me] and the life that You graciously gave me at first, for You are kind and patient. May You in Your kindness cause my prayer to rise before Your Throne of Glory. May my salvation reach Your Throne of Mercy and may my supplication and the words of my mouth find favor before You. And please, do not hide from my request, You Who were and will be forever. Please, God, command and have compassion on the work of Your

---

7. Noah, who lived ten generations after Adam is the first person called righteous by the Torah, as it says (Genesis 6:9) "These are the generations of Noah. Noah was in his generations a righteous man and wholehearted; Noah walked with God."

hands and let me understand and know what will happen to my descendants and future generations and what will become of me day by day and month by month. Do not conceal the wisdom of your ministering angels from me."

Adam's prayer was a request for prophecy. He wanted to know the future. And God answered him. Adam became a prophet.[8] His desire for prophecy was a desire for the revelation of God. God had spoken directly to Adam in the Garden of Eden, but now He spoke to him only through an angel. Sefer Raziel was intended to put Adam on the path that leads back to God and to true prophecy.

After the conclusion of Adam's prayer, *Sefer Raziel* continues with a narrative:

> After three days of prayer, the Angel Raziel came to him and sat by the side of the river that comes out of the Garden of Eden. He appeared to him toward the end of the day as the sun was setting. In his hand was a scroll. And he said to him, "Adam, why do you despair? Why are you so sad and worried? From the day that you stood up in prayer and supplication your words were heard. Now, I have come with pure understanding and great wisdom to make you wise with the words of this holy scroll. In them you will learn what will befall you until the day of your death. And every child of yours who fills your place and all later generations that conduct themselves according to this holy scroll with purity and an upright heart and a humble spirit will know what will happen to them in every month, day and night, and all things will be revealed to them. Now, Adam, draw close and turn your heart to the path of this scroll and its holiness."

---

8. The Midrash teaches that God showed Adam the future until the end of days. Adam saw a beautiful soul named David that was destined to be stillborn. Adam sacrificed seventy years of his own life so that David could live. But not only Adam was a prophet. The sages teach that all names are given by prophecy. Everyone who has a child and has given it a name has experienced prophecy, for all names are given by prophecy.

And the Angel Raziel opened the scroll and read it into the ears of Adam. When Adam heard the words of this holy scroll from the mouth of the Angel Raziel, he fell on his face in fear. And the angel said to him, "Adam, arise and be strong and do not be afraid. Take this scroll from my hand and guard it, for from it you will know and comprehend wisdom. Make it known to all who are worthy and it will be their portion."

As Adam took the scroll, a flame shot up from the river bank and the angel ascended in fire to heaven. And Adam knew that he was an angel of God and that the King had sent this book to strengthen him in purity and holiness.

Four generations later, the book was given to Enoch who used its wisdom to purify himself until he was like an angel. He immersed himself in a wellspring and concealed himself in a cave, meditating on the wisdom in *Sefer Raziel* until he understood his mission on earth.[9]

Enoch separated himself from all earthly beings and continued purifying himself until *"he was no more"*, for God had taken him into heaven and transformed him into the angel Metatron, the heavenly prince who supervises the angelic overseers. From here we learn that, in the Presence of *Hashem*, the God of Israel, there is no fixed destiny. There is no limit what people can attain. They can even become angels.

Part Two: Chaos and Salvation.

After Enoch, *Sefer Raziel* was concealed until Noah arose, a righteous man in his generations.[10] At that time, a cry of anguish went up to heaven before God's Throne of Glory, *"for all flesh had corrupted its way upon*

---

9. This shows that for one who follows the Torah, there is no such thing as fixed "karma." For in His great mercy, God elevated Enoch above his natural destiny.

10. Noah was Enoch's great-grandson. Enoch's son was Methuselah, whose son was Lamech, whose son was Noah.

the earth."[11] The time had come for God to destroy the creatures He had made. But Noah found grace in the eyes of the Lord.

The name Noah in Hebrew means rest or comfort, as his father, Lamech, said at Noah's birth, *"This one shall comfort us in our work and in the toil of our hands, which comes from the ground that the Lord has cursed."* [12]

Noah comforted mankind by inventing the plow and other farming implements, affording man rest from working the earth with his bare hands.[13]

Noah was a master craftsman. His skill and ingenuity improved the quality of human life. From Noah, we learn that a measure of the righteousness of man is his compassion for people and his ability to turn compassion into deed. This is the world of action[14] and if compassion does not become deed, it is of small value. Through his compassion and craftsmanship, Noah had the merit to be saved from the Flood, along with his family and a remnant of earth's species.

Craftsmanship is essential for a Noahide's ethical and spiritual growth in the world. Craftsmanship is being defined here as skilled labor that makes or improves a product, such as Noah's invention of farming tools. A Noahide can attain liberation and enlightenment through his craft. As a craftsman, he or she can go almost anywhere on Earth and he will always have garment and bread, as it says (Psalms 128:2), *"When you eat from the efforts of your hands, you will be happy and it will be well with you."* The craftsman will always have bread and clothing.

---

11. Rashi: The primary sins were idol worship, theft, and sexual immorality, three of the Seven Noahide Laws.

12. Genesis 5:31. The naming of Noah was, indeed, prophetic as we will soon learn.

13. Ibid., Rashi

14. According to Kabbalah, there are four spiritual worlds: *Atzilut* (Emanation), *Briah* (Creation), *Yetzirah* (Formation), and *Assiah* (Action), which is our world, the lowest of the four and the only world with the physical components of time and space.

The wise men of the east speak of craft as a form of meditation in action. It is raw power. Through years of practice, the craftsman's toil as a potter, carpenter, glazier, butcher, etc., becomes mentally and physically effortless. His hands execute intricate movements without need for his mind to consciously control them. When a butcher is an apprentice, he has to consider where to cut the thigh bone to separate it from a leg bone, often missing the mark and shattering the bone. But after practice and experience, the butcher does not have to consider where to cut. He just cuts. And the cut is perfect every time.

When the craftsman loses self-consciousness as he works his craft, he enters a meditative state. He becomes empty and attains oneness with his craft and the product of his craft, and the materials and tools with which he works. The master craftsman raises his awareness until he perceives his unity with all things and the unity of existence. From here, he can come to realize the Oneness of God. In Zechariah 1:20, the prophet speaks about four craftsmen who are brought by God to terrify the enemies of Israel.

There is no greater imitation of God than to be a craftsman, for God is the consummate craftsman. He created the world.

 The angel Raphael came to Noah in a dream and gave him *Sefer Raziel*. Noah meditated on its words and letters until the Spirit of the Lord rested upon him and he was prophetically shown how to build the Ark.

Noah and his wife and his three sons and their wives and the creatures of the earth, animals, birds, reptiles, fish and insects, two by two and seven by seven, were led into the Ark and saved from the raging waters of the Flood.

And Noah blessed God, saying, *"Blessed is the Lord Who gives of His wisdom to those who fear His Name and saves the souls of His Hasidim."*[15] From the wisdom of *Sefer Raziel*, Noah learned how to feed and care for all the creatures on the Ark. He understood the movements of the heavens and the months and seasons on earth. And Noah prayed to

---

15. *Sefer Raziel,* page 3. *Hasid* in the singular. This Hebrew word literally means a person who does kindness, but it implies piety as well.

God Who sent a wind over the earth and dried up the waters of the Flood. And the Ark rested on Mount Ararat.[16]

Noah was steeped in Torah learning. [17] He knew the laws of sacrifice. He knew which animals were spiritually clean and which were not, as it says,[18] *"Noah built an altar unto the Lord and took of every clean beast and of every clean fowl and offered burnt offerings on the altar."* He knew and observed the Torah's agricultural laws, as it says, *"And Noah, a man of the earth began and planted a vineyard."*[19]

Before Noah entered the Ark, God made a covenant with him. It is the first time the word 'covenant' (*brit*) appears in the Torah.

The Covenant before the Flood.

Genesis 6:17-21

Behold, I am bringing the Flood of water upon the earth to destroy all flesh that has in it the breath of life, from under the heavens. All that is on the earth shall perish. But I will establish My covenant with you, and you shall come into the Ark, you, and your sons and your wife and your sons' wives with you. And from every living creature of flesh, you shall bring into the Ark two of every kind to keep them alive with you, they shall be male and female. Of the fowl after their kind, and of the animals after their kind, of every creeping thing of the ground after their kind, two of every kind shall come to you to keep them alive. [20]

The covenant was God's promise that He would save Noah and all the creatures aboard the Ark from destruction by the Flood. It was given

---

16. Located at the eastern extremity of Turkey, near the border of Armenia, about 1200 km northeast of Jerusalem as the pigeon flies.

17. Genesis 7:2, Rashi on the verse.

18. Genesis 8:20.

19. Rashi: He had taken cuttings of the vine into the Ark with him.

20. Genesis 6:17-21.

unconditionally and implied that God would make another covenant with them after the Flood.[21]

The Rainbow Covenant.

After Noah survived the Flood, God made a second covenant with him.

Genesis 9:8-17:

And God spoke to Noah and to his sons with him, saying: "As for Me, behold, I establish My covenant with you and with your seed after you. And with every living creature that is with you, the fowl, the cattle, and every beast of the earth with you; with all that go out of the Ark, even every beast of the earth. And I will establish My covenant with you: never again will all flesh be cut off by the waters of the Flood, nor will there be another flood to destroy the earth."

At this time, God explained the sign of the rainbow: And God said:

"This is the sign of the covenant which I make between Me and you and every living creature that is with you, for everlasting generations. I have put My bow in the cloud and it shall be for a sign of the covenant between Me and the earth. And it shall come to pass when I bring clouds over the earth and the bow is seen in the cloud, that I will remember My covenant between Me and you and every living creature of all flesh, and the waters shall no more become a flood to destroy all flesh. And the bow shall be in the cloud, and I will look upon it that I may remember the everlasting covenant between God and every living creature of all flesh that is upon the earth."

God made two covenants with Noah. The covenant before the Flood eased his mind and lessened his fears as he was about to enter a stormy sea in a big wooden box surrounded by countless creatures that trample, bite and sting human beings.

---

21. Genesis 6:18; Ibn Ezra, Ramban, Rashbam

When Noah and his family emerged alive from the Ark, they knew that God had fulfilled His first covenant. They saw that He was more powerful than the forces of nature. He was God Almighty, a righteous Judge Who had shown them mercy. He loved them and wanted to care for them.

Now that God fulfilled his first covenant, Noah and his family were able to accept the second covenant with complete trust. Trust in God was essential here. They were being told to rebuild a world that had been destroyed. Logically, they might think that building for the future was sheer folly. Why rebuild a world in which man would sin again and God would destroy again?

But now that God made a new covenant with man guaranteeing that He would never again destroy their world, they could plant and harvest and be fruitful and multiply knowing that their future was secure. The two covenants provided them with a window into God's faithfulness and goodness, so that they could incorporate trust in God in their daily lives. And so it is with us today.

The Rainbow.

The *Mishnah*[22] tells us that the rainbow was created on the first Sabbath eve at twilight.[23] This imbues the rainbow with unique holiness. There are two blessings that one may say upon seeing a rainbow in the sky:

Blessed are You, Lord our God, King of the universe, Who does the work of creation.

Blessed are You, Lord our God, King of the universe, Who remembers the covenant, is trustworthy in His covenant, and fulfills His word.

---

22. Avot 5:8

23. According to the Torah's account of the six days of creation, the day begins at night, as it says (Genesis 1:5), *"And there was evening that was morning, day one."*

The Zohar teaches, *"Whoever stares at a rainbow is as though he stares at the Shechinah. And it is forbidden to stare at the Shechinah."*[24]

Since the rainbow has such radiant beauty as to be compared to the revealed Presence of God, there is concern that a person might fix his gaze upon it and experience such ecstatic joy that his soul would leave his body. Therefore, we are warned not to stare at a rainbow for long periods of time and not to call a friend to look at a rainbow. But we certainly are encouraged to look at it ourselves, appreciate it, marvel at its beauty, and bless God for having created it. And we can contemplate its nature as a metaphor for the Divine.

Scientifically, a rainbow is formed when a ray of sunlight strikes drops of water and is reflected as seven colors: red, orange, yellow, green, blue, indigo, violet. The British physicist Sir Isaac Newton demonstrated that the same effect occurs when a beam of white light is projected through a glass prism. The white light splits into seven colored lights. Isaac Newton also discovered that when the seven colored lights are projected through a second prism, they are refracted back again as white light. This means that hidden within every ray of white light are seven colors. This is a great secret of creation.

A similar concept is taught regarding the *Menorah* in the Holy Temple. The *Menorah* is a seven-branched candelabrum fashioned out of a single block of gold. When lit, the *Menorah* has seven flames, but only one light emanates from it. By meditating on the phenomenon of the *Menorah* and the nature of the rainbow, one can attain enlightenment.

Noah the Saint (*Tzadik*).

Noah is often characterized as a benign old grandfather with a giraffe smiling down at him from a window in the Ark. That is not Noah. That is the kindergarten version of Noah. The real Noah is a dazzling white light of Torah, a spiritual giant among spiritual giants. He was the Crown of Torah before the Torah was given on Mount Sinai. In the entire Chumash only two beings are referred to as a '*tzadik*' (saintly person). One is Noah.

---

24. Zohar, Beshallach 66b.

The other is God Himself, as it says, "*A God of faithfulness and without iniquity, righteous (tzadik) and upright is He.*"[25]

King Solomon wrote (Proverbs 10:25), "*Tzadik yesod olam, a righteous person is the foundation of the world.*" Mankind had shown itself to be so wicked and corrupt that God was moved to blot out man from the face of the earth. "*But Noah found grace (chen) in the eyes of the Lord.*"[26]

All of mankind was judged for destruction, except for the perfectly righteous Noah. And in Noah's merit, God saved him and his family, and all the species of creatures on earth.

Noah was salvation. But salvation was not enough. Mankind also needed redemption. And Noah did not provide this. Abraham did.

Salvation means being rescued from evil. Redemption means being returned to God in purity and holiness. The problem is that salvation and redemption are two separate realms without a connection. The interface between Noah's salvation and Abraham's redemption was Shem, the righteous son of Noah.

Part Three: The Torah of Shem.

The Torah of Shem begins with *tzedaka*. *Tzedaka* means righteousness, but it is often translated as charity, giving of oneself for the betterment of others. *Tzedaka* refers to helping people by giving them money, but it includes every type of help, even a kind word. The *mitzvah* of *tzedaka* is so great that throughout the Jerusalem Talmud it is called "*The Mitzvah.*"

The Kabbalists teach that *tzedaka* brings man to perfection, merging salvation with redemption. Noah originated it. Shem taught it. And Abraham perfected it. Wisdom has no other purpose than to accomplish *tzedaka*.

What was the *tzedaka* that Noah practiced? He and his family fed and cared for all the animals, birds and creatures aboard the Ark. They worked around the clock with little or no sleep, caring for every species of creature on earth.

---

25. Deuteronomy 32:4

26. Genesis 6:7,8.

When Shem emerged from the Ark, he reasoned that if God had wanted him to practice *tzedaka* with animals and birds, all the more so he should practice *tzedaka* with human beings. So he taught Torah to show people how to merit God's blessings in the new world. This was his *tzedaka*. It led him to establish the Academy of Shem and Eber, the first yeshiva in the world, the first school of any kind. Among Shem's illustrious students were Abraham, Isaac, and Jacob, Job, Balaam and countless scholars, judges, mystics, and prophets.

Shem taught the whole Torah to Abraham including the mystical teachings of *Sefer Raziel*.[27] He taught him the full depth and breadth of the Seven Laws of Noah. According to the Talmud, Abraham studied 400 chapters of Torah law about idol worship. Most important of all, Shem taught Abraham the *mitzvah* of *tzedaka*.

Abraham was lovingkindness clothed in a human body. He fed people, clothed them and housed them and set them up in business, and taught them to care for others. He brought thousands of people under the sheltering wings of the Shechina. He elevated them to the level of Gerim. And this, too, was considered tzedaka.

God loved Abraham and blessed him with all good things because he practiced *tzedaka* and taught his children to practice *tzedaka*.[28] It had begun with Noah caring for animals and was perfected by Abraham performing deeds of lovingkindness for all mankind in the Name of God. And the Torah of Shem was the vessel for this light.

The Rambam teaches that giving *tzedaka* is the identifying mark of a righteous person. Therefore, we should be more concerned about *tzedaka* than any other positive mitzvah in the Torah.[29] Throughout the Jerusalem Talmud, *tzedaka* is shown to be equal in importance to Torah learning, as exemplified by the relationship between Zebulon and Issachar, two brothers and sons of Jacob. Issachar was a great scholar and judge. Zebulon was a successful merchant seaman who supported Issachar in his Torah learning, for which he received half of Issachar's reward.

---

27. Genesis Rabba, 43:6.

28. Genesis 18:19.

29. Mishneh Torah, Laws of Charity 10:1

No person ever became impoverished because of giving *tzedaka*, as it says (Proverbs 28:27), *"He who gives to a poor man will lack nothing."* In fact, giving *tzedaka* will bring wealth to a person.[30] Every coin that a person gives to *tzedaka* is an investment in the World to Come. And during one's earthly life, there is no evil force that *tzedaka* cannot defeat, as it says, *"Whoever acts with mercy receives mercy in return."*[31]

The Rambam[32] teaches that there are eight basic levels of giving tzedaka:

1. The highest level, above which there is none higher, is to support a brother Israelite by endowing him with a gift or loan, or entering into a partnership with him, or finding employment for him, in order to strengthen his hand until he need no longer be dependent upon others, as it says, "And if your brother grows poor and his means of support fails with you, then you shall strengthen him, a Ger and a Toshav shall live with you."[33] As the saying goes, "Give a man a fish and you feed him for a day; teach him how to fish and you feed him for the rest of his life."

2. A lower level of tzedaka than this is to give to the poor without knowing to whom you give, and without the recipient knowing his benefactor. This is performing a mitzvah solely for the sake of Heaven. It is like the anonymous fund that was in the Holy Temple. There, the righteous gave secretly and the righteous poor received secretly. Giving to a charity fund is similar to this, though one should not contribute to a charity fund unless one knows that the fund is administered by

---

30. Babylonian Talmud, Taanit 9a, Tosefot...asser.

31. Mishneh Torah, Laws of Charity 10:2.

32. Ibid. 10:7-14.

33. Leviticus 25:35. This verse includes the Ger Toshav (Noahide) in the category of Israel with respect to his right to receive tzedaka if he lives on the land (Ibn Ezra). If the Ger Toshav can receive tzedaka, then all the more so should he give tzedaka if he is able.

responsible, wise and trustworthy people, like Rabbi Chananyah ben Teradion.[34]

3. A lower level of charity than this is when one knows to whom he gives, but the recipient does not know who his benefactor is. There were great sages who would walk about in secret and place coins in the doors of the poor. It is worthy and good to do this, particularly if those who administer charity funds are not trustworthy.

4. A lower level of charity than this is when one does not know to whom one gives, but the recipient knows his benefactor. The greatest sages used to tie coins in linen cloths and throw them behind their backs. The poor would come up and take the coins out of the cloths so that they would not be ashamed.

5. A lower level than this is when one gives directly in the hand of a poor person, but gives before being asked.

6. A lower level than this is when one gives to a poor person after being asked.

7. A lower level than this is when one gives less than is fitting, but gives gladly and with a smile.

8. A lower level than this is when one gives grudgingly.

The Talmud[35] tells about the time Rabbi Akiba had a visit from a Chaldean astrologer who told him that on the day his daughter enters the bridal chamber, a snake will bite her and she will die. Rabbi Akiba was alarmed by this. On the day of her wedding, his daughter took a hairpin and stuck it between the stones of the wall. The pin sank into the eye of a snake. The following morning, when she took the hairpin out from between the stones, the snake fell onto the floor, dead.

"What did you do to merit this?" her father asked.

---

34. Rabbi Chananya ben Teradion was a second century rabbi who administered a charity fund so scrupulously that, one time, his own money designated for use on *Purim* got accidentally mixed in *tzedaka* funds, so he gave it all to the poor.

35. Babylonian Talmud, Shabbat 156a.

"A poor man came to our wedding party last night," she replied, "and everybody was busy at the banquet, so there was no one to help him. That is when I took the portion that was given to me and gave it to him."

"You have done a *mitzvah*," he said to her. Afterwards, Rabbi Akiba went out and lectured, "Tzedaka delivers from death and not merely from an unnatural death, but from death itself."

Concerning *tzedaka*, there are two verses from the Prophets that work together: *"Listen to Me, you hard-hearted that are far from tzedaka,"*[36] and, *"I will take away the heart of stone from your flesh*[37] *and I will give you a heart of flesh."* This is the Ger who has been delivered from the raging Floodwaters of Noah to the Lovingkindness of Abraham, and who understands the true meaning of *tzedaka*, as it says (Isaiah 32:17), *"The act of tzedaka will be peace, and the service of tzedaka will be tranquility and security unto Eternity."* And making *Gerim* is the ultimate *tzedaka*, for it gives life to the poor in spirit.

Part Four: The Tents of Shem.

Noah blessed his sons, saying, *"Blessed be the Lord, the God of Shem, and let Canaan be their servant. God increase Japheth and he shall dwell in the Tents of Shem."*[38]

Wherever the knowledge of God is being learned, there you will find the Tents of Shem. Noah was a completely righteous man in his generations, but Shem's righteousness spans all generations.

The *Arizal*[39] teaches that a tent is part garment and part house. It has the qualities of both because it contains the essence of both. This is

---

36. Isaiah 46:12.

37. Ezekiel 36:26

38. Genesis 9:26,27

39. Rabbi Isaac Luria Ashkenazi (1534-1572), considered the greatest of Kabbalists, who received the tradition directly from the mouth of Elijah the Prophet. The vast body of his teachings were given over to his primary talmid, Rabbi Chaim Vital, in Tsfat during the two years, 1571 and 1572.

the spiritual level of *Keter* (Crown), the Source of the *Sephirot*, where Emanator and emanation exist as One.

The Tents of Shem include every yeshiva that ever was or ever will be. The Tents of Shem include the tents of Abraham and Sarah, the tents of Jacob, the tent of Moses, the Tabernacle and the Holy Temple.

The *Shechinah* (Divine Presence) dwells only in the Tents of Shem.[40]

The Torah of Shem can be understood by looking at the Tent wherein it all began, namely, the Yeshiva of Shem and Eber. Every religious Jewish child knows that Rebecca went to the Yeshiva of Shem and Eber to consult with the prophets about her difficult pregnancy with Jacob and Esau. And every one of them knows that Jacob learned in the Yeshiva of Shem and Eber for fourteen years on his way to find a wife in Paddan-Aram. But ask any child or adult what was learned in the Yeshiva of Shem and Eber or anything about the yeshiva at all, and hardly one will be able to tell you because the nature of the Torah of Shem is hidden. No matter how revealed it appears to be, it is hidden.

We do know, however, that the Yeshiva of Shem and Eber taught prophecy. There was another yeshiva that taught prophecy: the *B'nei Neviim* (School of Prophets) under the leadership of Elijah the Prophet and the Prophet Elisha. Like the Yeshiva of Shem and Eber, the *B'nei Neviim* are hidden. Rabbi Abraham Ibn Ezra says that they were meditators. We know virtually nothing else about them.

Ohr HaGanuz (The Hidden Light).

Rabbi Joseph Karo, author of the *Shulchan Arukh* (Code of Jewish Law), said that the Torah of Shem is the *Ohr HaGanuz*, the Hidden Light, and the light of the House of David.[41]

On the first day of creation, when God said, *"Let there be light,"* it was not a physical light. The sun and the moon were not in the heavens until the fourth day. It was the holy light of the *Shechina*, the revelation of God. This radiant light continued shining until the night following the

---

40. Rashi from Midrash Rabba on Genesis 9:27

41. Magged Meshorim, Vayeshev

first Sabbath when it was hidden away for the righteous. This is the *Ohr HaGanuz*, the Hidden Light.

The Midrash says that Noah was mauled by a hungry lion that was not fed on time. And so, Noah's son Shem ran to the Garden of Eden to get a cure for his father's wounds. While in the Garden, he ate from the Tree of Life and drank from the wellsprings that water the Tree of life.

Shem returned with a healing balm for his father. And he also returned with the Torah, which is the Tree of Life, as it says (Proverbs 3:18), *"It is a Tree of Life for those who grasp it."*

The Torah that Shem received in the Garden of Eden was the *Ohr HaGanuz* and the light of the House of David, light that is hidden for the righteous. There is a Baal Shem Tov[42] story that relates to this exalted level of Torah:

Rabbi Dov Ber of Mezeritch heard the great reputation of the holy rabbi, the Baal Shem Tov, and about the throngs of people who were always traveling to him, and the wondrous and great things that his prayers accomplished.

Now, Rabbi Dov Ber was a brilliantly gifted Torah scholar. He had mastered the Talmud and all the commentaries, and had ten hands of the wisdom of Kabbalah. And yet, he was amazed by the reports of the lofty spiritual level of the *Besht*.[43] So he made up his mind to journey to him and test him.

Rabbi Dov Ber studied Torah constantly. But when he was on the road for a day or two, it became impossible for him to focus on his learning as when he was in his own office, so he began to regret having made the trip.

Finally, he reached the *Besht* and expected to hear words of Torah from him. But the *Besht* told a story about how he was once traveling many days and there was no bread left to give to his wagon driver. And so he found a poor man with a sack of bread and purchased enough bread to satisfy the hunger of the wagon driver. He told several other stories like this one.

The next day Rabbi Dov Ber came again to the Baal Shem Tov. This time he told him a story about how he was traveling on the way and the

---

42. Rabbi Israel ben Eliezer (1698-1760), the father of the Hasidic Movement. Baal Shem Tov means master of a good name.

43. An acronym for Baal Shem Tov.

feed for the horses became spoiled. So he hunted around until he found a poor man with a sack of feed.

The secret truth is that each of the stories that the Baal Shem Tov told had great wisdom and wondrous revelations hidden within them for those who understood. But Rabbi Dov Ber did not understand them.

Rabbi Dov Ber returned to the inn where he was lodging and said to his servant, "I want to travel home tonight, immediately. But because it is a particularly dark night, we will wait until the light of the moon appears and then we will be on our way."

Around midnight as Rabbi Dov Ber was preparing to travel, a servant of the Baal Shem Tov came to the inn to bring him back to the *Besht*. He was disgruntled, but he obliged the servant.

When he arrived, the Baal Shem Tov asked him if he knew how to learn Torah. Rabbi Dov Ber answered, "Yes."

The Baal Shem Tov said, "Yes, I heard that you know how to learn."

And then the *Besht* asked him if he had any knowledge of the wisdom of Kabbalah. And he said, "Yes."

The *Besht* said to his servant, "Bring Sefer *Etz Chaim*[44] to me."

The servant retrieved a large volume from the bookcase. The *Besht* opened it and showed a specific passage to Rabbi Dov Ber, and asked him to explain the simple meaning of the passage. Rabbi Dov Ber studied the passage, considered its meaning, and then explained it.

The *Besht* said to him, "You know nothing."

Rabbi Dov Ber picked up the book again and read the passage carefully, then said, "The interpretation is correct the way I said it. If you have a better explanation, please tell it to me and I will be pleased to hear the truth."

The *Besht* said to him, "Stand upon your feet." And he stood. That particular passage contained the names of many angels. The moment the *Besht* began reciting it, the house became filled with light and heavenly fire surrounded them, and they beheld with their physical sight the angels as they were being named.

The Baal Shem Tov then said to Rabbi Dov Ber, "The interpretation you gave was a true one the way you said it, but your learning lacked a *neshama* (soul)."

---

44. The Book of the Tree of Life, the magnum opus of the Arizal as written down by Rabbi Chaim Vital.

Immediately, Rabbi Dov Ber ordered his servant to return home while he remained with the Baal Shem Tov to learn by him. Eventually, he became his disciple and successor. This story was heard from the mouth of Rabbi Dov Ber, the Maggid of Mezeritch.[45]

And the Baal Shem Tov taught, *"Let your path always be towards Hashem."*

This is the Torah of Shem. It is not only a map, but also the territory.

Soaring with Noahide Torah.

Noahide Torah is different from Israelite Torah insofar as Israelite Torah is a physical Torah and Noahide Torah is a spiritual Torah. [46]

Israelite Torah is a physical Torah in that enables the Jew to raise the physical world to *kedusha* (holiness). For example, the Torah instructs the Jew to take four species of vegetation – an *etrog* (citron), a *lulav* (palm frond), three *hadassim* (myrtle twigs) and two *aravot* (willow twigs) – bundle them together and shake them during the festival of Sukkot. The Jew shakes them east and west, north and south, up and down, and by doing so nullifies the physical world to holiness by fulfilling a *mitzvah* of the Torah. The same dynamic is true of many *mitzvot* – eating *matzah* on Pesach, writing a Torah scroll with ink on parchment, lighting Shabbat candles and making *kiddush* over a cup of wine. [47]

Noahide Torah is a spiritual Torah in that it stands apart from the physical world. There are no *mitzvoth* for *B'nai Noah* to fulfill by using a physical object. The Seven Laws of Noah do not raise the world to *kedusha*. They earn reward for the Noahide in this world and the Eternal World. The Noahide's basic mission is to refrain from worshipping idols, refrain from murdering people, refrain from stealing things, etc., and he gets a share of Eternal Life as a reward. By all standards, this is a pretty good deal. But it

---

45. Kesser Shem Tov, Part II, page 23a.

46. There is only one Torah. Israelite Torah and Noahide Torah are two aspects of the one Torah.

47. Lighting Shabbat candles and making Kiddush over a cup of wine are rabbinic enactments.

is incomplete, for it does not allow the Noahide to soar on spiritual wings while he is in a body in this physical world.

However, there are two ways a Noahide can elevate the physical world (including himself) to holiness. One is by attaining prophecy. The other is by bringing a sacrifice to the Holy Temple.

The Noahide brings his little goat to the Temple. The Kohen (Jewish priest) takes it from him, inspects it, then offers it on the *Mizbeyach*, the Great Altar, in the Noahide's name. The goat's flesh, hair, skin, and bones are transformed from mundane animal matter to holiness of the highest degree. And the Noahide's soul soars on high with the savory scent of the column of smoke. The Seraphim of *Briah* (Creation), the world of the Throne of Glory are nurtured by his offering.[48]

Sadly, there is no Temple standing in its place in Jerusalem. But God is good. In the same manner that the Noahide teamed up with the Kohen to bring his sacrifice, he can team up with any Jew to do any *mitzvah*, and his soul will soar on high as when he offered his sacrifice in the Temple. This is the secret of Zechariah 8:23, *"So said the Lord of Hosts: In those days, ten men of all the languages of the nations will take hold of the corner of the garment of a Jewish man, and say, 'Let us go with you, for we have heard that God is with you.'"*

The "corner of the garment" is the *tzitzith* (knotted strings) which are tied on each of the garment's four corners, *"And it shall be as a fringe for you, so that you may see it and remember all the commandments of the Lord and perform them."*[49]

The Torah of Shem and Abraham.

The other avenue of spiritual ascent available to the Noahide is the path of prophecy. To walk this path, a person must refine his thoughts,

---

48. Mishkanay Elyon by Rabbi Moshe Chaim Luzzatto, the Ramchal, zy"a.

49. Numbers 15:39. The numerical value of tzitzit in Hebrew is 600 plus eight strings and five knots on each corner adds up to 613, the number of mitzvot of the Torah. Also, the color of the blue string placed on each corner reminds one of the sea which reminds one of the sky, which reminds one of the Throne of Glory.

speech, deeds and physical body to become a vessel for the Godly Light. This opens his channel of Divine communication and keeps it open, as artist Peter Max taught, *"The goal is not to work on the painting, but to work on the place within you that lets the painting come through."*

According to the Rambam, *"Prophecy is bestowed only upon a very wise man of strong character who never gives in to his animal desires and is physically sound."*[50] This does not negate the teaching that all names are given by prophecy.

Sefer Yetzirah – The Book of Creation.[51]

Just as the Yeshiva of Shem and Eber was the first school in the world, so was *Sefer Yetzirah* (the Book of Creation) the first book of Torah.[52] *Sefer Raziel* is older, but *Sefer Raziel* does not fit into the accepted tradition of Torah because it came from the hand of an angel. Authentic Torah comes from two sources only: From Moses at Sinai and from Elijah the Prophet.[53] The sole exception is *Sefer Yetzirah* which predates Sinai by four hundred years.

Sefer Yetzirah is accepted as authentic because great sages have established Abraham as its author.[54] According to Rabbi Eliezer Rokeach's[55] classic commentary on *Sefer Yetzirah*, Shem taught Abraham many of

---

50. Mishneh Torah, Laws of the Foundations of Torah 7:1.

51. A more accurate translation of Sefer Yetzirah is The Book of Formation. Creation implies creating something from nothingness. Formation implies giving form to some elemental substance, such as forming man out of the dust of the earth.

52. The mystical teachings of the Torah.

53. Shaarei Avodah, the Strasheler Rebbe, introduction

54. Pardes Rimonim, 1:1.

55. Rabbi Eliezer of Wurms (1165-1230)

the early traditions that eventually became the six short chapters of *Sefer Yetzirah*.[56]

Rabbi Aryeh Kaplan called *Sefer Yetzirah* the oldest and most mysterious of all Kabbalistic texts. His translation and commentary[57] is the most comprehensive in the English language. Aryeh Kaplan's viewpoint is that *Sefer Yetzirah*, when properly understood, becomes an instruction manual for a form of meditation that strengthens concentration and *"aids the development of telekinetic and telepathic powers."* This is certainly akin to prophecy.

Sefer Yetzirah is part of the oral tradition. The six chapters are divided into sixty-two brief teachings, which were transmitted orally from teacher to student from Shem to Abraham and from Abraham to Isaac and so forth until the second century C.E., when Rabbi Akiba is reputed to have redacted the various existing versions as a single cohesive text.

Excerpts from Sefer Yetzirah:

Chapter 1:1:

With 32 wondrous paths of wisdom *Yah*, the Lord of Hosts, the God of Israel, the living God and King of the universe, *El Shaddai*, Merciful and Gracious, High and Exalted, Dwelling in Eternity, Whose Name is Holy, Lofty and Holy is He, did engrave and create His world with three books: with text, with number, and with communication.

Commentary:

The 32 paths: are the ten Divine Emanations (*Sephirot*) and twenty-two Letters [of the Hebrew alphabet].[58]

Wondrous: above human comprehension.

---

56. Sefer Rokeach (Jerusalem 1967), p. 19

57. Published by Samuel Weiser, Inc.

58. Shaarei Tzedek (commentary on Sefer Yetzirah), p.16

Engrave: God "engraved" a constriction in His Eternal Light and created the world within that constriction.

Text: the Letters of the Hebrew alphabet

Number: numbers 1 through 9 and 0.

Communication: Words formed of letters, and calculations using numbers (dates, distances, etc.), stories, lessons, and laws.

Chapter 1, Mishna 8:

Ten *Sephirot* of nothingness. Bridle your mouth from speaking [of them] and your heart from thinking. And if your heart runs, return to the Place. Therefore, it is written (Ezekiel 1:24), "And the *Chayot* (Angels) ran and returned." Concerning this a covenant was made.

Commentary:

Sephirot: The *Sephirot* are the attributes of God, may He be blessed, that He manifests for the needs of created beings, for no attributes exist with respect to His perfection and essential existence.[59]

nothingness: without form or substance; beyond the grasp of human intellect.

bridle your mouth: speaking or thinking about the *Sephirot* physicalizes them, for man thinks in physical terms. However, it is possible to meditate on the *Sephirot* and experience them.

the Place: God, may He be blessed, is the Place of the world.

the Chayot: A category of angels.

---

59. Rabbi Moses Chaim Luzzatto, zy'a, Sefer Clalim 1:1.

ran and returned: spiritual growth is described as running to God and returning. Running to God strips away the mundane. Returning brings down blessings and holiness from God, may He be blessed.

Abraham: the beloved of God.

Noah is the biological father of everyone on earth. Abraham is their spiritual father. Noah brought them into this world. Abraham delivered them to the World to Come.

Abraham did not limit his service of God to the Seven Laws of Noah. Even though the revelation at Sinai would not come for another four hundred years, Abraham, through prophecy and the tradition he received from Shem, was able to observe all 613 mitzvot of the Torah.[60] Abraham was the father and role model of all *Gerim*, as the Ramban taught,[61] *"The deeds of the fathers are signposts for the children."*

God raised Abraham above the angels. After Adam sinned he fell under the supervision of the guardian angels of the nations of the world. The Talmud[62] tells us that Adam was fed roast meat by the angels. This meant that Adam's sustenance came from angels, not directly from God. This was not the case with Abraham.

Three days after Abraham had been circumcised, three angels in the guise of human travelers appeared in front of his tent. Abraham, in pain from the circumcision, left off speaking to God, and ran to greet the visitors. Abraham so loved the *mitzvah* of providing food and lodging for travelers, that he put aside his physical pain to offer hospitality to these strangers. Abraham fed the angels butter and calf's tongue and mustard and unleavened bread, for it was Passover. And the angels ate Abraham's food. This was a great miracle, for angels do not eat earthly food. Angels are entirely spiritual without a digestive system that would permit them to

---

60. And some say the rabbinic decrees and injunctions.

61. Commentary to Genesis 12:6.

62. Sanhedrin 59b.

eat food. And yet, God caused the angels to transcend their nature and eat earthly food, to show that, in the future, the sustenance of the angels will come from the Jewish priests, who are Abraham's seed and who will offer sacrifices to the God of Israel in the Holy Temple.[63]

Abraham was a master astrologer. He knew that his and Sarah's destiny, their *mazal*,[64] was to go childless. But God, may He be blessed, raised Abraham and Sarah above their natural destiny. Originally, their names were Abram and Sarai. God then added a letter *Hay* to Abram's name and he became Abraham, and He exchanged the letter *Hay* for a *Yud* in Sarai's name and she became Sarah, as it says, *"And God said to Abraham: as for your wife Sarai, you shall not call her name Sarai, but Sarah shall be her name. And I will bless her and I will give you a son from her; yes, I shall bless her and she shall be a mother of nations; kings of populaces shall be from her (Genesis 17:15,16)."*

The *mazal* of Abram and Sarai was to go childless, but the *mazal* of Abraham and Sarah was to give birth to a son, Isaac. And Isaac begat Jacob, Jacob begat Levi, Levi begat Kehot, Kehot begat Amram, and Amram begat Moses and Aaron and Miriam. And the people went out of Egypt into the wilderness with Moses and camped at Sinai. And a new covenant was established between God and Israel. And the *Gerim* were given a share in it, as it says (Deuteronomy 10:17), *"Love the Ger, for you were Gerim in the land of Egypt."*

Melchizedek: the perfect king and priest of God.

Shem appears to play a minor role in the Biblical narrative, but the truth is that he is a prime activator and energizer of Israel and the *Ger*. Most important is the flow of Divine energy between Shem and Abraham, which is the interface between Chaos and Order, and comes only from *El Elyon*, God Most High, the Name of God that indicates Lovingkindness and

---

63. Mishkanay Elyon, Rabbi Moshe Chaim Luzzatto, the Ramchal, zy"a.

64. This is similar to the Natural fate, what the Hindus call karma. It is a system of justice without mercy. The God of Abraham directs the world with both justice and mercy, and a justice that is also merciful.

Mercy without any Judgment at all, absolute and total redemption from which there can be no falling.

The Book of Genesis[65] tells us that in the days of Abraham, war broke out between four kings and five kings. Abraham's nephew, Lot, was in the wrong place at the wrong time and was captured by the four invading kings, who plundered the wealth of Sodom and Gomorrah and went on their way.

When Abraham heard what happened, he mustered a militia of 318 men from his household.[66] They pursued the four kings, defeated them in battle, rescued Lot and brought back the spoils of war. This was a formidable, even miraculous, show of strength that aroused the admiration of the surrounding Canaanites.

As they were returning from the battle, Abraham and his homespun army rested in the Valley of Shaveh outside the walls of Jerusalem.

Melchizedek, the king of Jerusalem and a priest of God Most High, brought bread and wine to the battle weary Abraham and his men. This same Melchizedek was the first one to build a wall around Jerusalem.[67]

From the Book of Genesis 14:18-20:

14:18: And Melchizedek, King of Salem, brought out bread and wine; and he was priest of *El Elyon*, God Most High.

14:19: And he blessed him, and said, *"Blessed is Abram of God Most High, Possessor of heaven and earth."*

14:20: *"And blessed be God Most High who delivered your enemies into your hand."* And he [Abraham] gave him a tenth of all [the booty].

This meeting of Melchizedek and Abraham is more than an historic moment. It opens the channel of God's bestowal of freedom and holiness to the world forever.

---

65. Genesis 14:1-17

66. Genesis 14:14

67. Seder Dorot 9b

And who is this Melchizedek, the first king and the first priest mentioned in the Torah? He is none other than Shem, the son of Noah, wearing the garments of kingship and the priesthood.[68]

From the Zohar Chadash:[69]

The Holy One, blessed be He, took Shem the son of Noah and made him the priest of God Most High to serve Him, and His *Shechina* rested upon him. And He called his name Melchizedek, King of Salem. And his brother, Japheth, learned Torah from him in his *yeshiva*. And then Abraham came along and taught Torah in the *Yeshiva* of Shem. And the Holy One, blessed be He, turned His attention to Abraham and forgot all the others. So Abraham prayed before the Holy One, blessed be He, that His *Shechina* should always dwell in the House of Shem, and He consented, as it says (Psalms 110:4), *"You are a priest forever according to My word, Melchizedek."*

There is an opinion in the Talmud[70] stating that, because Melchizedek blessed Abraham before he blessed God, the priesthood was taken away from him as a punishment and given to Abraham.

The *Ohr HaChaim*[71] disagrees and maintains that Melchizedek conferred the priesthood upon Abraham willingly.

It is difficult to make sense of this. The fact is that that Melchizedek never lost the priesthood and Abraham never received it. After Melchizedek, the next person mentioned in the Torah as a priest is Aaron,

---

68. Targum Yonatan, Genesis 14:18-20; Babylonian Talmud, Nedarim 32b.

69. Zohar Chadash, Parshat Noach p.22 (Sulam)

70. Babylonian Talmud, Nedarim 32b.

71. His commentary on Genesis 14:19. Rabbi Chaim ben Attar (Ohr HaChaim 1696-1743) was a Moroccan Talmudist and Kabbalist who wrote a major commentary on the Chumash.

the brother of Moses. Aaron is a descendant, son after son, of both Abraham and Shem.[72]

We can answer the opinion that maintains Melchizedek blessed Abraham before he blessed God. It is possible to say that Melchizedek actually blessed God first.

Let us look again at Genesis 14:19. It reads: *"And he blessed him, and said, 'Blessed be Abram of God Most High, Possessor of heaven and earth.'"*

The *Ohr HaChaim* maintains that if this were only one blessing, it would read, *"And he blessed him, **saying**..."* But since it is written, *"And he blessed him, **and said**..."* It indicates that *"**And he blessed him**,"* is one blessing, and *"**said**..."* is a separate blessing.

Once we have established, *"And he blessed him,"* as its own blessing, it logically refers back to God Most High in the previous verse, as one can plainly see:

14:18: And Melchizedek, King of Salem, brought out bread and wine; and he was priest of *El Elyon*, God Most High.

14:19: And he blessed Him (God Most High)... and he said, *"Blessed is Abram of God Most High, Possessor of heaven and earth."*

Therefore, Melchizedek blessed God first, made no error, and did not lose the priesthood.

The Torah itself testifies that Melchizedek could not have been punished for blessing Abraham no matter how he did it, as it says (Genesis 12:3), *"And I will bless them that bless you and I curse him who curses you."* Can we then say that Melchizedek blessed Abraham and was cursed for it?

The explanation is that there are certain nodules along the path to the *Messiah* that must appear in a negative light in order to make progress in this world of darkness. This is the Lot and his daughters program and the Judah and Tamar program, where the lineage of *Messiah* had to come through a circuitous path.

---

72. Abraham is a ninth generation, son after son, descendant of Melchizedek. Therefore, Abraham's descendants are also Melchizedek's descendants.

Melchizedek's blessing was advertised as a failure to send a message to the "unclean powers" that says, *"Why bother with this insignificant, failed blessing? Go do your dirty work elsewhere in greener pastures."*

But truth be told, it was Melchizedek's blessing that prepared the way for Abram to become Abraham and Sarai to become Sarah. And his blessing continues from generation to generation, preparing the Abram and Sarai within each one of us to be raised up as Abraham and Sarah. And it is Melchizedek, the Righteous Priest (*Kohen Tzedek*), who is Shem and who will anoint Messiah as King of Israel, may it happen soon in our days.

✡ ✡ ✡ ✡

It is because of the Torah of Moses that we even know the names of Shem or Noah, or Adam, Seth and Enoch. Without the Torah of Moses, there are only the flood myths of extinct civilizations. So it is obvious that the Torah of Shem exists solely because of the Torah of Moses. But, at the same time, it is the Torah of Shem that fully awakens the heritage of Sinai, as it says (Leviticus 26:45), *"But for their sakes I will remember the Covenant of the Ancients, for which I brought them out of the land of Egypt in the sight of the nations, that I might be their God; I am the Lord."*

Commentary:

Covenant of the Ancients: Adam, Seth, Noah, and Shem (*Midrash Rabba on Leviticus 26:45.*).

In the sight of the nations: When the nations remember the Covenant of the Ancients, they will awaken and turn to the Lord as their God, may He be blessed.

I am the Lord: When all the nations come to the God of Israel, then the Lord will be One and His Name One, and His Kingdom will rule the entire earth, as it says (Isaiah 2:3), *"And many peoples will go and say, 'Come, let us go up to the mountain of the Lord, to the House of the God of Jacob and He will teach us of His ways and we will walk in His paths.'"*

This is *Olam Ha-Rachamim*, the World of Mercy, where nature can be altered and there is no judgment, only a continuous stream of *Chesed* (Kindness) emanating from *El Elyon*, God Most High, may He be blessed.

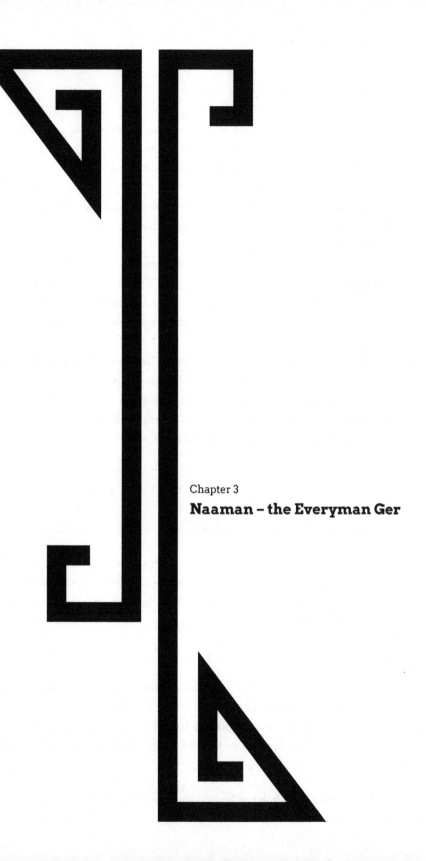

Chapter 3
Naaman – the Everyman Ger

The Story of Naaman[1]

Naaman[2] was the name of a general in the Aramean army during the First Temple period, when the Jewish people were divided into two kingdoms, the kingdom of Judea and the kingdom of Israel.

Naaman was a great man in the eyes of his people, the Arameans. Besides being a general and a great warrior, Naaman was the close and trusted aide of the king of Aram.[3] But Naaman's life was far from perfect; he was afflicted with leprosy.[4]

Naaman became a hero to his people when God gave the Arameans a military victory over Israel through him. As the battle began, Naaman randomly shot an arrow in the air. It struck and killed Ahab, the king of Israel, causing the Jewish troops to scatter and flee, giving the victory to Aram.

Around the same time, the Arameans had sent raiding parties into Israel. One of them captured a young Jewish girl, who became a servant of Naaman's wife. When the girl saw that Naaman was a leper, she said to her mistress, "My master should go to the prophet who is in Samaria[5] and plead with him, and he will cure him of his leprosy."

---

1. The account of Naaman is found in the Second Book of Kings, Chapter Five.

2. The name Naaman in both Hebrew and Aramaic means 'pleasant.' It is the masculine counterpart of Naomi (Naamah), the name of the mother-in-law of Ruth and the name of the wife of Noah, both significant personages in the world of the Ger.

3. The Biblical Aram is present day Syria.

4. In Hebrew, zaraath. Zaraath can mean either leprosy or a unique affliction that can be diagnosed and healed only through the agency of the Jewish priesthood, as explained in Leviticus, chapter 13. It is unclear which form of the disease is meant here, but we have translated the word as leprosy, since the severity of that affliction is well known.

5. Samaria was in the heart of the kingdom of Israel, approximately 50 km north of Jerusalem.

Naaman came before the king of Aram and told him what the girl had said. The king answered, "Go, and I will send a letter to the king of Israel on your behalf." Naaman immediately prepared to travel to Israel, taking with him ten talents of silver, six thousand gold pieces and ten silk tunics.

The letter from the king of Aram was delivered to the new king of Israel. It read, "Behold, I have sent my trusted servant, Naaman, to you and you are to cure him of leprosy."

After reading the letter, the king of Israel tore his clothing and cried out, "Do I have the power of God to put to death and bring to life that this one sends a man to me to cure his leprosy? This is just a pretext to go to war against me."

When Elisha, the man of God, heard that the king of Israel had rent his garments, he sent word to the king, saying, "Why have you torn your clothing? Let that man come to me so he will know that there is a prophet in Israel."

Thus, Naaman came to the house of Elisha, leaving his servants and companions at a distance, and coming alone on horseback to Elisha. He stood at the doorway of his house and announced his presence. Elisha sent a messenger to him who told him, "Go and immerse yourself seven times in the river Jordan and your flesh will be restored and you will be healed."

Naaman was furious. He had come all that way with many attendants bearing precious gifts, and Elisha had not even spoken to him personally, but only through a servant.

Naaman said, "I imagined that he would come out to see me and he would call in the Name of his God, YHVH, and he would raise his hand and point his finger towards me and cure my leprosy. Are not Amanah and Parpar, the rivers of Damascus, better than all the waters of Israel? Would I not become clean if I immersed myself in them?" And he turned and went away in a rage.

But his servants approached and spoke to him, saying, "If the prophet had given you a difficult task to perform, would you not have done it? And yet, all he told you to do is immerse yourself in the river and become healed."

Naaman realized the truth of their words and went and immersed himself seven times in the Jordan according to the word of the man of God. And his flesh returned to flesh like a young boy's. He became pure. He was healed.

Naaman returned to the man of God, he and his entire entourage, and he stood before him and said, "Behold, now I know that there is no God in all the earth except with Israel. And now, please accept this gift from your servant."

And Elisha said, "As the Lord lives[6] before Whom I have stood, I will not accept it." Naaman pressured him to take the gift, but Elisha refused.

And Naaman said, "Then please permit your servant to be given a load of earth carried by a team of mules, for your servant will no longer offer up a burnt-offering or any sacrifice to other deities, but only to the God of Israel. And for one thing may the Lord forgive your servant: when my master the king comes to Beth-Rimmon[7] to prostrate himself there, and he leans on my hand, I must prostrate myself in Beth-Rimmon alongside the king, may the Lord forgive your servant for this thing."

Elisha answered him with his blessing and said, "Go in peace.[8]"

After Naaman had departed and traveled some distance away, Gehazi, the disciple and assistant of Elisha the man of God, thought, "My master has refused Naaman the Aramean by not taking from his hand what he had brought as a gift. As the Lord lives, I will run after him and take something from him." And Gehazi chased after Naaman.

When Naaman saw Gehazi running after him, he stepped down from his chariot to greet him, asking, "Is all well?"

Gehazi answered, "All is well. My master sent me, saying, 'Just this moment, two young disciples of the prophets have come to me from Mount Ephraim. Please give them a talent of silver and two silk tunics.'"

Naaman said, "Please, take two talents." And he tied two talents of silver in sacks and the two silk tunics, and gave them to his servants who took them to Gehazi.

---

6. An expression of an oath.

7. The temple of a pagan deity.

8. In Hebrew, Lech L'shalom. This is the same blessing that Jethro gave to Moses upon his departure to confront Pharaoh in Egypt. It literally means "go towards peace," but we use the English vernacular. See Chapter 5, Jethro, the legacy of a Ger.

Gehazi went to a secret place and took the items from the servants' hands,[9] hid them in his house, and then dismissed the servants. Afterwards, he came and stood before his master.

And Elisha asked, "From where did you come, Gehazi?"

And he answered, "Your servant has been nowhere special, just here and there."

And Elisha said to him, "Did my heart not follow you when the man descended from his chariot to greet you? Did you see this as your chance to take silver and precious garments and with them buy olive trees and vineyards and flocks and herds and servants and maidservants? Now, your reward shall be that Naaman's leprosy shall afflict you and your children forever." And Gehazi went away, stricken with leprosy, white as snow.

The Naaman Program.

The Bible's account of Naaman is more than a story with real people and historical events. It is an allegory that forms the pattern for every *Noahide Ger*. Every *Ger* can see himself in Naaman, for every *Ger* experiences the Naaman Program.

The story of Naaman, the Everyman *Ger*, begins before we meet him in the Book of Kings. We do not see the beginning. The beginning takes place in heaven before Naaman is born. It begins with God choosing the soul of a *Ger* and bringing it into the world. In this particular case, the soul is Naaman who is born into an idol-worshipping family in Syria. It appears that Naaman[10] is in the process of rejecting idolatry and choosing God. But the truth is that it is God Who chooses Naaman because He knows that Naaman will choose God. It is a love story.

At a certain point in the Naaman program, this love becomes manifest. In the very beginning of the story in the Second Book of Kings, the love

---

9. According to Rashi, Naaman was suspicious of Gehazi. So he had his servants accompany him to see if he was telling the truth.

10. From this point forward, the name Naaman refers to the both the historical Naaman and the generic *Ger*.

becomes manifest when a miracle happens for Naaman. He enters battle against the previously invincible forces of Ahab, the wicked King of Israel.[11]

Ahab had never lost a battle. Many scholars are puzzled by this. Why should an idol worshipping Jewish king be granted repeated victories in war? This is particularly strange when one considers that Saul, a righteous Israelite king, lost many battles.

And it was not merely Saul who was righteous. His soldiers were righteous. And Ahab's soldiers were idolaters whose lives were, therefore, forfeit.

Ahab and his men may have been wicked, but they had great souls. And Saul's men, righteous though they were, had souls of lesser stature. What was the practical difference? Tolerance. Because they had great souls, Ahab and his men loved each other and allowed for the shortcomings of each other. Saul and his men, by contrast, were judgmental and many despised each other. And victory in war is determined in heaven by one human trait alone, unity, *achdut* in Hebrew, which requires harmony and tolerance for each other.

Against this background of Israel's invincibility, the Aramean general Naaman enters battle. He places an arrow in his bow, draws back the string to its fullest and lets it fly aimlessly into the air. And the arrow finds King Ahab, piercing his armor, mortally wounding him and ending the battle. The army of Israel abandons the battlefield and heads for home. The Arameans were victorious. God had chosen the *Ger* to be the instrument of victory in a miraculous way.

Naaman as well as everyone else on the battlefield could choose to believe the event was a miracle or he could think that it was *mikreh*, a coincidence. But even if every other soldier on the field considered the event to be just plain old good luck, Naaman knew the truth. This is the *Ger's* awakening. He sees the hand of God at work. He has *gilui Shechina*, the revelation of the Divine Presence. He has become aware that God has chosen him. This is the essence of the Everyman *Ger* Program. God reveals Himself to Naaman and Naaman realizes it. And it will continue to

---

11. *"Ahab did that which was evil in the eyes of the Lord more than all before him (I Kings 16:30)."* Ahab married Jezebel a non-Jewish heathen. Together, they introduced the worship of Baal to Israel.

happen until Naaman makes a life changing decision to abandon idolatry and accept the ways of the Torah and walk in His paths.

Naaman is stricken with leprosy. It is this affliction that leads directly to his redemption. His leprosy is phase two of the Everyman Ger program. Not all Gerim are afflicted as severely as Naaman, but something always separates them from their immediate environment. They no longer feel like the rest of the members of their family or friends. They no longer think the way others think. They are no longer able to worship the way others worship.

The Ger has become a different being, a leper in his own eyes, and his estrangement will not go away. If he were to divulge his radical thoughts, other people might try to talk him out of them or tell him he needs a psychiatrist or call him a heretic. God is communicating with him and people are threatened by this. The tikun (rectification) of this is the search to find a prophet in Israel, even though the Talmud[12] tells us that prophecy has been lost to Israel since the early days of the Second Temple period, some 2400 years ago. This appears to be a paradox.

One of the most notable examples of this dilemma was Joan of Arc, a fifteenth century farm girl who at the age of eighteen led France in battle against England, claiming that the voice of God was instructing her to lead her country's army to victory. And she proceeded to win an amazing series of military victories. In the end, the Church condemned her as a heretic and burned her at the stake for claiming that God spoke to her.

Every Ger is a threat to the status quo of an idolatrous society. It is this alienation that forces the Ger to take refuge in God and moves him onto the path of love.

Now comes the third phase of the Everyman Ger program – the Jewish moment. In Naaman's case, a young Jewish girl was kidnapped by Arameans and brought to Damascus where she became a servant in Naaman's household. Every Ger has a Jewish moment. And it can recur again and again.

The Jewish moment may take place in a park or at the supermarket or anywhere. At the very moment when the person is having a spiritual thought, someone will step up wearing a Star of David or his eyes will fall on a newspaper featuring Israel in the news. It is God reinforcing the Ger's

---

12. Babylonian Talmud, Baba Batra 3a.

thoughts by connecting him with something Jewish. At least, this is how the Ger views it. Disinterested parties might see this as mere coincidence. The Ger sees it as Divine Providence.

God told Elijah the Prophet atop Mount Sinai that of the millions of Jews living in the northern kingdom of Israel, only seven thousand did not worship the Baal.[13] But the Jewish girl that the Arameans kidnapped just happened to be God fearing (another apparent coincidence). She tells Naaman's wife that there is a prophet of God in Israel and that Naaman should go to him and he will heal his leprosy. And it will be by a miracle because leprosy was incurable.

The revelations and the Jewish moments are beginning to fit together like the pieces of a puzzle. Naaman could have ignored the girl's bizarre suggestion, but instead he acts by going to his friend, the king, and telling him what the Jewish girl said. Surprisingly, the king of Aram, a long time enemy of Israel, writes a friendly letter to the king of Israel asking him to cure Naaman. The Ger is on the way. He is off to see Elisha, the disciple of Elijah, the great miracle worker.

Of course, not every Ger has to seek a prophet to be put on the path of loving God. (After all, according to the Talmud, prophecy has been hidden from Israel for nearly 2500 years.) The Ger of today will meet a religious Jew or he will begin looking at Jewish internet websites and get Torah insights about upcoming Jewish holidays, such as Passover or Chanukah, or the Sabbath. In this world of instant worldwide communication and mobile phones, the Jewish moment is right in front of everyone's face. Naaman the Ger has now become a vessel to begin to receive the Light of God.

So General Naaman takes ten talents of silver, six thousand gold coins and ten silk tunics as gifts for the prophet. Why ten talents and ten tunics? Why six thousand coins? Numbers have profound meaning for the Ger. Ten Commandments. Six thousand years of creation. Every number can now be seen as a code, a message from God. And, indeed, the code is real and the message is real.

Naaman travels with a large retinue to Elisha and he is treated shabbily. Elisha does not even come out to greet him, but sends a servant who tells Naaman to go and dunk in the Jordan River seven times. Seven!

---

13. I Kings 19:18.

Another number. But seven is not just another number. Seven is a very special number. Seven days of the week. Seven colors of the rainbow. Seven shepherds.[14] And most significant of all, the Seven Laws of Noah. Seven is a charmed number. "All sevens are beloved" is a classic Hasidic saying.

Elisha has humbled the great Aramean general, taking him down hard from his inflated ego. God says, "There is room inside this man for only one of us, either him or Me." The humiliation at the hands of the prophet is a part of the program. The Everyman *Ger* might call a rabbi who has no time for him or he might actually show up at a synagogue to pray along with the Jewish people and be ignored or snubbed by the congregation. Or worse, they might suspect him of being a missionary and ask him to leave. God loves to test the *Ger*. Every test is drawing him closer with cords of love, as it says (Psalm 23:4), *"Your rod and Your staff comfort me."*

And this is the real reason that Elisha does not even speak directly to him. The prophet wants the healing to be between Naaman and God Himself. If Elisha were to place his hands on Naaman and heal him directly, there might be room for error. Naaman might presume that the prophet himself performed the miracle. The true prophet of God is concerned only for the glory of God. The true prophet flees from fame and honor. Elisha wants this Gentile to come to his Father in heaven not to himself. He wants Naaman to reject idolatry.

How amazing it is that the Jewish people never made a god out of Elijah the Prophet, Elisha's master, the only man in Scripture to have ascended to heaven in the flesh without first dying. Or Moses. Think about it. No one ever worshipped Moses! How is that possible? The man who split the Red Sea and did not eat or drink for forty days on Mount Sinai, and yet his people never worshipped him or made him into an avatar. The true prophet of Israel does not take the glory of God for himself. And so, Elisha communicates with Naaman through a messenger until the miraculous healing is completed so that Naaman will know that it is God Who heals him, and not Elisha.

But the Everyman *Ger* is angry about the way Elisha ministered to him. He had risked traveling into enemy territory and was humiliated for his troubles. No one ever treated this powerful general and confidant of the king in such a manner. All of Naaman's pre-conceived notions of what

---

14. Micah 5:5.

could or should happen are dashed to pieces. He has now entered the next phase of the *Ger* Program. He sees the Jew and Jewishness in a negative light. After all, even God Himself called them a stiff-necked people.[15] And what about the Jordan, that miraculous Jewish river? A third rate trickle by world standards. When the American author Mark Twain visited the Holy Land in 1867 and saw the Jordan River about which he had been reading in the Bible his whole life, he practically fainted. In his own words, *"When I was a boy I somehow got the impression that the river Jordan was four thousand miles long and thirty-five miles wide. It is only ninety miles long, and so crooked that a man does not know which side of it he is on half the time."*[16]

Mark Twain grew up on the banks of the Mississippi River which at one point is over two miles (3.2 km) wide. And in Israel, he saw a pathetic little stream that slows to a dribble and practically dries up completely in some places. You call this a river? Naaman wants nothing to do with it. He is ready to abort the mission. But God will not let go of him. No one can save a person out of the hand of God, not even the person himself, not even a Jewish prophet. This is all about God working with the *Ger*.

Naaman has come to that phase of his life where every occurrence, positive or negative, inspiring or demeaning, is a revelation of God. At the very moment that he wants to give up, Naaman's servants come to him and say, "Your attitude is wrong. What have you got to lose? If the prophet had told you to climb the highest mountain or fast for four days to be healed of leprosy, wouldn't you do it? And yet, all he did was tell you to dip in the Jordan River seven times. A piece of cake."

An Aramean general's servants talking to him like that is inconceivable. Chutzpah! They dare treat him like a fool or a child? He could have them killed for such insubordination. But no, Naaman has become a vessel for the light and he hears the truth. Maybe there is a reason that the Jordan is a little river. Did God not appear to Moses in a lowly bush? Was not Mount Sinai a humble little mountain? Maybe its smallness is what endears the Jordan to God.

---

15. Exodus 32:9.

16. Mark Twain, Innocents Abroad, Chapter 55.

So Naaman obeys the words of the prophet. He immerses himself in the Jordan precisely seven times and he is healed. His incurable leprosy is gone. His flesh has become pure and wholesome, like that of a young boy. God has performed a miracle for him. God has chosen Naaman and now He has openly revealed to Naaman that He has chosen him.

At some point in the program, every Ger sees that God has chosen him, as it says (Jeremiah 3:14,15), *"And I will take you, one from a city and two from a family and bring you to Zion. And I will give you shepherds according to My heart and they will feed you with knowledge and understanding."*

Finally, we have a miracle that cannot be denied or confused with coincidence. It is a life changing event.

Naaman and his attendants return to the house of Elisha, who this time comes out to greet him. And Naaman says, "Behold, now I know that there is no God in the world except with Israel." He has renounced idolatry. According to an opinion in the Talmud,[17] this alone qualified Naaman to be a Ger Toshav with the right to reside in the land of Israel and be supported by the Jewish community. The rejection of idolatry is the defining moment in the life of every Noahide *Ger*.

Now, how does Naaman attempt to show his appreciation? By giving *tzedaka*.[18] Naaman has a giving heart, the finest of all human traits.[19] And the mitzvah of giving *tzedaka* has actually been grafted onto the body of the Seven Noahide Laws.[20] So the Everyman *Ger* offers Elisha a generous gift, but he promptly turns it down. Naaman pleads with him to take it,

---

17. Babylonian Talmud, Avodah Zara, 64b, the opinion of Rebbe Meir. But this is not the law. To qualify as a *Ger Toshav*, one accepts all seven Noahide laws.

18. The Hebrew word for charity is *tzedaka* actually means righteousness and there are sages who are displeased with its translation as charity. Charity implies an act done gratuitously from the goodness of one's heart, whereas *tzedaka* implies that it is fitting for a person to share with others the wealth given to him by God.

19. Chapters of the Fathers 2:13.

20. *The Path of the Righteous Gentile,* Chapter Thirteen.

but Elisha is adamant and swears by the Name of God that he will accept nothing to diminish the purity of what has happened.

Elisha wants no material reward for his righteousness. Bringing an idol worshipper to true faith in God is itself the greatest reward imaginable. Rebbe Nachman of Breslev taught that bringing a Gentile from idolatry to faith in the God of Israel is the greatest of all spiritual accomplishments.[21] Elisha needs nothing from Naaman except the knowledge that he has delivered his precious soul to its Maker, the Lord of the universe.

Naaman changes the subject and requests something from Elisha. He asks for permission to take a wagon load of earth in order to build a sacrificial altar back home in Damascus. This is another defining moment. By showing his respect for the soil of the land of Israel, he demonstrates his love of the land and his respect for God and the Jewish priesthood. The Baal HaTurim[22] writes, *"Phineas and Hofni, the two sons of Eli, the High Priest, desecrated the priesthood by their actions, whereas Naaman showed his respect for the priesthood by building his sacrificial altar from the earth of the land of Israel. In the end, Phineas and Hofni were killed for their misdeeds and Naaman was brought under the wings of the Shechina and his grandsons become great scholars of the Torah."*

By asking Elisha's permission to take the soil, Naaman demonstrated that he had become scrupulously observant of the Noahide prohibition against theft. He has not merely rejected idolatry, but has taken upon himself the entire doctrine of the Seven Noahide Laws.

And now, Naaman brings to Elisha a problem he must face. It is a problem that every Noahide *Ger* must deal with in some form or another. Sooner or later, the Noahide will return home to live among idol worshippers. These are his people. He loves them and must remain at peace with them. So Naaman asks Elisha that God should forgive him for returning to his previous way life, because he is going to live it as a pretense. The issue centers on the king of Aram, under whose dominion

---

21. Likutei Moharan, Torah #14.

22. Commentary to Exodus 28:7. The *Baal HaTurim* is Rabbi Jacob ben Asher (1268-1343), author of an esoteric commentary to the *Chumash* and the *Arbaah Turim*, the prestigious work of *halacha* that formed the basis of the *Shulchan Arukh* (Code of Jewish Law).

Naaman must live. As the king's trusted aide, one of Naaman's duties is to accompany the king when he visits the temple of the local Aramean god. The last place on earth that Naaman wants to be is in a temple of *avodah zara* (idol worship). But the king requires it of him and when the king bows down before his idol, Naaman will be expected to bow along with him. But in his heart, Naaman will be bowing only to the God of Israel.

Elisha blesses him with, *"Lech l'shalom - go towards peace,"* meaning that God will be with Naaman now and forever, even in times of danger and places of darkness.

The spiritual filth that Naaman grew up with is no longer part of him. The foreskin of his heart has been circumcised. And so, Naaman departs from Elisha, prepared to be a lonely man of faith, a ray of light in the midst of darkness.

Now, the *Ger* Program takes an unexpected turn. Gehazi, Elisha's disciple and assistant, enters the scene. Gehazi is not a man of God like Elisha, his master. In fact, Gehazi is a predator. He knows that Naaman is as innocent as a child who only wants to do the right thing. Gehazi sees his chance to benefit from this, because Naaman is wealthy and has brought a fortune in gold and silver with him.

Gehazi pursues Naaman and swindles him out of a prodigious sum of money, deceiving Naaman by conjuring up a total lie. And he tells the lie in the name of Elisha, saying, "My master sent me, saying, 'Just now two young men have come to me from Mount Ephraim. They are disciples of the prophets. Please give them a talent of silver[23] and two silk tunics.'"

Still flush with joy and feelings of generosity, Naaman says to Gehazi, "Please, take two talents." Naaman's freewill offering is profoundly symbolic. It is as if he spoke prophetically without realizing it. Torah scholars, and all the more so disciples of the prophets, are compared to the gold-plated wooden beams that formed the walls of the Tabernacle Moses built at Mount Sinai. Under every wooden beam of the Tabernacle were two massive silver sockets, each weighing one talent. The silver sockets were forged from half-shekel donations given by the Children of Israel as a redemption for their souls, as it says, *"And the Lord spoke to Moses, saying, 'When you take the sum of the children of Israel according to*

---

23. A talent is 42.5 kilograms of silver, worth approximately $30,000.00 in 2014 dollars.

their number, each man shall give a ransom for his soul to the Lord when you number them, that there be no plague among them (Exodus 30:11,12).'"

Naaman has symbolically offered a two-talent silver ransom for his soul. From his standpoint, this is all good. Even though he was swindled, Naaman has fulfilled the *mitzvah* of giving *tzedaka*.

But all is not well with Gehazi. Naaman suspects that Gehazi is lying, but gives anyway.[24] Gehazi has desecrated the Name of God by implicating the Prophet Elisha in his deception.

And so, Naaman returns home, his body purified and his soul redeemed by the God of Israel as it says, *"Thus says the Lord, 'You are my witnesses and My servant whom I chose, in order that you know and believe Me and understand that I am He; before Me no god was formed and after Me none shall be. I, I am the Lord, and besides Me there is no savior (Isaiah 43:10,11).'"*

As for Gehazi, his sin was very great. Elisha prophetically saw exactly what Gehazi did, and says to him, "Now, Naaman's leprosy will cling to you and to your children forever." And Gehazi slinks away, stricken with leprosy.

The Mishna[25] tells us that Gehazi was one of four commoners who were punished by losing their share of the Eternal World. The four are Baalam, Doeg, Achitofel and Gehazi. Baalam maliciously caused a plague that took the lives of 24,000 Israelites. Doeg murdered 500 *Kohanim* (Jewish priests) because they had fed a starving King David. Achitofel advised Absalom to rape David's concubines in public view to show that he was now the king. And Gehazi swindled Naaman out of some money and clothing.

Gehazi does not seem to belong in that group of truly evil men. Gehazi was greedy and foolish. The others were monsters.

But the truth is that Gehazi *does* belong there with the others. Gehazi gave Naaman an excuse to believe that Jews are greedy, money-hungry predators. Gehazi's greed and foolishness has brought shame to Elisha and

---

24. Midrash Samuel 15.

25. Sanhedrin 11:1

to the entire Jewish people. There is no greater desecration of God's Name than this.

Gehazi serves as a warning for future generations: Be careful with the Ger. God loves the Ger and, therefore, so should you, as it says, *"Love the Ger for you were Gerim in the land of Egypt (Deuteronomy 10:19)."* This Ger is Naaman, a foreigner who sojourned among Israelites like the Israelites sojourned among the Egyptians. And when he returned home, he became a righteous Gentile, a Ger, among idolatrous Arameans.

Chapter 4
Jethro – the Legacy of a Ger

Exodus 1:8-10:

"Now there arose a new king over Egypt who knew not Joseph. And he said to his people, 'Behold, the people of the Children of Israel are too many and too mighty for us. Come, let us deal wisely with them lest they multiply and it come to pass that if a war should occur, they may join our enemies and fight against us and go up from the land.'"

Pharaoh and the Egyptians enslaved the Israelites and afflicted them with harsh labor. But the people grew stronger and more numerous. Then Pharaoh's astrologers told him that a Hebrew child would be born who was destined to liberate the Israelites and destroy Egypt. So Pharaoh plotted to kill the newborn male infants. But before he put this evil plan into effect, he consulted with his three chief advisors to see what they thought about it.

These three advisors were Balaam, Job and Jethro. The wicked Balaam enthusiastically supported the idea and advised Pharoah to drown every male Israelite infant as soon as he was born. Job remained silent, refusing to advise Pharaoh either way. Only Jethro objected to the plan and insisted that Pharoah abandon it. He continued to protest until Pharoah decided to have him arrested and executed. Jethro discovered the plot against him, and he fled to Midian.[1]

With Jethro out of the way, Pharaoh ordered his soldiers to cast the newborn Hebrew male babies into the Nile and allow the baby girls to live.[2]

When the baby Moses was born, they hid him for three months. But because his crying would be heard, they placed him in basket and set him afloat in the Nile. Pharoah's daughter rescued him and raised him as a prince of Egypt.

When Moses learned that he came from Hebrew stock he went out to see his enslaved people. He saw an Egyptian taskmaster beating one of his Hebrew brothers. Moses struck down the Egyptian and buried his body in the sand.[3]

---

1. Exodus Rabba 1:9.

2. Exodus 1:22.

3. Exodus 2:11,12.

Pharoah heard about the matter and sought to have Moses killed, but Moses fled to Midian and sat by the side of a well.

Now, Jethro who had run away from Pharoah a generation earlier had settled in Midian. As one of Pharoah's ex-advisors, he was appointed as the high priest of the Midianite idol, *Baal-Peor*. The Talmudic term for such an idol worshipper is an *acum*, the Hebrew acronym for "one who serves stars and constellations."

But as Jethro grew older, his meditations and natural goodness led him to question his belief in idols. With this change of consciousness, he was no longer an *acum* and had become a *nochri* or a *ben nechar*, a stranger.[4] A *nochri* is a person who is still connected to his idolatrous upbringing, but has serious doubts and keeps one foot out the door.

Loss of faith in the Midian idol caused Jethro to resign his priesthood. This resulted in the Midianites banishing him as a heretic, for it is the way of the world to ostracize a person who rejects his religious upbringing. He has become an apostate and threatens the belief system of his family and community. If they cannot convince him to return to their faith, he often becomes an outcast.[5]

Jethro was forced to live at the edge of the wilderness away from society with no means of survival except to raise sheep and goats. It was at this phase of his life that Jethro worshipped every god known to him in order to find his way to the truth. That is precisely when Divine Providence became revealed to him.

Jethro had seven daughters and no sons. His daughters shepherded Jethro's flocks just as Laban's daughter, Rachel, had been a shepherdess 300 years earlier. This shows that Jethro had lost his wealth and influence. If he had been able to afford servants, the servants, rather than his daughters, would have been his shepherds.

Shunned and despised as they were, Jethro's daughters were driven away from the watering well by the local shepherds. This was the same

---

4. A *nochri* may have begun to search for the truth, but he has not accepted the Seven Laws of Noah.

5. This may not be a firm rule in today's world where atheism is so widespread and considered even worse than worship. In times of danger, it is preferable to seek shelter in the house of an idol worshipper than that of an atheist.

well where Moses was sitting. Moses came to the daughters' rescue by driving off the shepherds and watering Jethro's flocks.

The daughters returned home to their father, Reuel (one of Jethro's seven names). He asked them why they returned home early this day. They told him that an Egyptian saved them from the shepherds and watered their sheep.

Jethro was upset by their lack of kindness in abandoning one who had helped them. He told them to bring the man home to break bread with them.

Moses was treated with such warm hospitality that he agreed to live with Jethro. Jethro gave his daughter Zipporah to Moses as his wife.[6]

Zipporah gave birth to a son and Moses named him Gershom, saying "I was a stranger (*Ger*) in a foreign (*nochria*) land." Later, Moses had a second son, who he named Eliezer, meaning God is my helper.

One can only wonder about the mystical and ethical discussions that these two great souls, Moses and Jethro, engaged in during the years that Moses lived with his father-in-law.[7] Here was the greatest of all Jewish prophets and the former High Priest of Midian exchanging their views of God and life.

The Parable of the Staff

Jethro possessed the mystical staff that had been given to Adam in the Garden of Eden. The staff had God's Name engraved on it and whoever possessed it inherited the true wisdom of God.[8] The staff was reputed to have been made of sapphire or of a heavenly stone resembling sapphire.

---

6. Exodus 2:17-21.

7. There is a tradition that Moses was in Cush (Ethiopia) for forty years and became a king there. Then he was thrown into a dungeon for another ten years. This would still leave twelve years that he lived with Jethro, for it is taught that Moses fled from Pharaoh when he was eighteen years old and returned to free the Jewish slaves when he was eighty.

8. This was the original *Kabbalah*, which means "receiving" in Hebrew.

Adam gave the staff to Enoch.[9] Enoch gave it to Shem, the son of Noah. Shem gave it to Abraham. Abraham gave it to Isaac and Isaac gave it to Jacob. From Jacob it went to Joseph. When Joseph died, Pharaoh confiscated all of his belongings including the mystical staff. Jethro knew that whoever had the staff would receive the true wisdom of God. Jethro wanted that staff. He also knew that Pharaoh had stolen it from Joseph's sons, Ephraim and Manasseh, robbing them of their inheritance, which included the staff, so it really did not belong to the Egyptian king. When Jethro fled Egypt over the issue of killing the Hebrew babies, he seized the staff and took it with him. After he got to Midian and set up his household, Jethro used his powers of *kishuf*[10] to thrust the staff into the ground so that no one could remove it except its rightful owner. He then let it be known that whoever could pull the staff out of the ground would be given Zipporah as his wife.

Zipporah was extraordinarily beautiful and all the young men of Midian tried to pull the staff out of the ground to win her as his bride, but no one could budge it. One day, Moses came into Jethro's courtyard and saw the staff. He noticed that there was Hebrew writing on it. To get a better look at the words, he pulled the staff out of the ground and took it to Jethro to find out what the writing meant. Jethro immediately realized that Moses was the one chosen to receive the wisdom of God and to marry Zipporah.

Moses' Mission

Moses began shepherding Jethro's flock. One time he led the flock to the edge of the wilderness and came to Mount Sinai, where he saw a bush that was burning but was not consumed by the fire. God spoke to Moses from out of the fire and charged him with the mission of bringing the Children of Israel out of Egypt to this mountain where they would be chosen by God as His holy nation.

---

9. Another version says that Adam gave the staff to his son, Seth, and Seth gave it to Enoch.

10. Kishuf is the Hebrew word for magic or witchcraft. As one of Pharaoh's advisors, Jethro along with Balaam were masters of occult wisdom, which included all forms of sorcery.

Moses returned to Jethro his father-in-law and said, "I must go to my brothers in Egypt to see if they are still alive." Jethro told him to leave Zipporah and his two sons behind because the situation in Egypt is dangerous. But Moses persisted and Jethro blessed him that he should arrive at his destination with shalom.

God then spoke to Moses' brother, Aaron, and told him to go out and meet Moses. The brothers met and embraced after a separation of more than sixty years.

Aaron saw Moses' wife and sons and said, "We are grieving over our loved ones in Egypt and you want to add to their number?" This time Moses took the advice and sent Zipporah, Gershom and Eliezer back to Jethro in Midian.

Moses and Aaron then traveled to Egypt to petition Pharaoh to free the Hebrew slaves. A year later, after God had struck Egypt with ten plagues and annihilated their military capability at the Red Sea, Moses led the Israelites to Mount Sinai where it all began.

The Sinai Experience.

Forty-six days after leaving Egypt, Moses and the Children of Israel and the mixed multitude of people who sought refuge with them arrived at the foot of Mount Sinai. The people's bodies had been purified by eating manna[11] and drinking water from Miriam's Well. The lame could walk straight and the blind could see as every physical defect was healed. The *zuhama*, the flow of spiritual filth that entered man when he ate from the Tree of Knowledge, ceased. And the people were raised above the grasp of death.[12]

The Israelite men had been circumcised before leaving Egypt. At Sinai, all the men and women immersed in the purifying waters of Miriam's Well. Moses told the people that if they listened to God's voice and kept His covenant they would become a kingdom of priests and holy nation to

11. The manna began to fall the morning of the 16th of the Hebrew month of *Iyar*, two weeks prior to people arriving at Mount Sinai.

12. Babylonian Talmud, Shabbat 146a.

God. And all the people answered, "All that the Lord has spoken we will do."

Moses and the young Israelite men offered sacrifices on behalf of the people. Half the blood was thrown onto the altar and the other half of the blood was sprinkled on the people, and Moses said, *"Behold the blood of the covenant."*[13]

The mountain became enveloped in smoke as God descended upon it in fire and the mountain shook with fear. The call of the shofar sounded and grew louder and louder as Moses went up and God came down upon the mountain, merging heaven and earth as one.

And then, God said all the words of the Ten Commandments. As God spoke, His words emanated from every direction, above and below, east and west, north and south. The people saw the words coming from their own mouths as well. God revealed to them that He is the only true existence.[14] This nullification to God sanctified the people and made them distinct from all other people on earth.

The Sinai experience was a transformation process which became the template for all future conversion. The process consisted of circumcision and ritual immersion for men, ritual immersion for women, offering a sacrifice in the Holy Temple, and a commitment to observe the commandments of the Torah.

There are two important questions here concerning Jethro:

1. Did Jethro convert and become a Jew or did he remain a Noahide throughout his life?

2. If Jethro remained a Noahide why did he choose to do so?

Jethro comes to Mount Sinai.

There is great significance in determining exactly when Jethro came to Mount Sinai. If he came before the Sinai Revelation, it is logical to presume that he became an Israelite along with the rest of the people

---

13. Exodus 24:5-8.

14. Reishit Chachmah, Sha'ar HaYirah.

who heard the voice of God pronounce the Ten Commandments. But if he came afterwards, he would have had to personally undergo the conversion process of circumcision, ritual immersion, offering sacrifices, and accepting the commandments of the Torah. But nowhere in the verses of the Torah or in the words of the Talmud do we find that Jethro performed any of these obligations, except for bringing sacrifices, which the verse does not indicate was for the sake of conversion.[15]

Since the Ten Commandments are found in the portion of the Torah called *Jethro*, it would seem that Jethro came to Mount Sinai at the same time as the Children of Israel, and that he heard the Ten Commandments and became an Israelite.[16] But the Talmudic sages disagree as to when Jethro arrived at Mount Sinai.[17] And there is strong evidence to show that Jethro came after the Sinai Revelation and did not convert to become an Israelite, but remained a *Noahide Ger* throughout his life.

To determine when Jethro arrived to Mount Sinai, we need to examine the pertinent verses in the Book of Exodus to see whether his arrival could possibly fit into the events of the first six days at Mount Sinai that led up to the revelation of God.

The first day: Arriving at the Foot of Mount Sinai

"In the third month of the Israelites' exodus from Egypt, on that same day they came to the wilderness of Sinai. (Exodus 19:1)"

This was the first day of the Hebrew month of Sivan, forty-six days after Moses led the people out of Egypt. On that day some 2,400,000 men,

---

15. Exodus 18:12.

16. It should be kept in mind that, prior to the Sinai Revelation, all the Israelites, even Moses, had the status of a Noahide in Jewish Law.

17. Babylonian Talmud, Zevachim 116a. Rabbi Yehoshua says he came before the Giving of the Torah and Rabbi Eleazar of Modi'm says he came after the Torah was given.

women and children, arrived at the foot of Mount Sinai and set up their encampments,[18] an all day event.

The Second Day: Moses Ascends the Mountain

From the Book of Exodus 19:3 - 19:8:

19:3: Moses went up to God. God called to him from the mountain, saying, "This is what you shall say to the house of Jacob and tell the children of Israel."

19:4: "You have seen what I did to Egypt and how I carried you on wings of eagles and brought you to Me."

19:5: "Now if you obey Me and keep My covenant, you shall be my own treasure from among all the peoples, for all the world is Mine."

19:6: "You will be to Me a kingdom of priests and a holy nation. These are the words that you are to say to the Children of Israel."

19:7: Moses came down and summoned the elders of the people. He presented these words to them as God had commanded him.

19:8: All the people answered as one and said, "All that God has spoken, we will do." And Moses brought the words of the people back to God.

The Third Day: Moses Ascends the Mountain Again

On the third day, Moses ascended the mountain once more[19] and God spoke to him again.

---

18. The figure of 2,400,000 is based on the explicit counting of 603,550 men between from age 20 and up (Numbers 1:46) then taking that number as one-fourth of the total population of older men, women, and children. This is a population equal to a city the size of Chicago or Toronto or Rome.

19. Mekhilta, Yalkut Shimoni.

19:19: And the Lord said to Moses, "Behold, I will come to you in a thick cloud so that the people will hear when I speak to you and they will also believe in you forever." And Moses told God the words of the people.

According to *Rashi*, the "words of the people" was the people's expressed desire to hear the communication direct from God and not through Moses.

The Fourth Day: The People Begin to Sanctify Themselves

On the fourth day, God spoke again to Moses.

Exodus 19:10 - 19:15:

19:10: God said to Moses: "Go tell the people and sanctify them today and tomorrow. Let them wash their clothing."

19:11: "Let them be ready for the third day.[20] For on the third day, God will descend on Mount Sinai in the sight of all the people."

19:14: Moses descended from the mountain to the people. He sanctified the people and they washed their clothing.

19:15: Moses said to the people, "Keep yourselves ready for the next three days. Do not touch a woman."

On the fourth day, Moses taught the people some of the commandments of the Torah. He explained the Seven Laws of Noah and commanded the Israelites to teach these laws to the other nations. He also reviewed the

20. The "third day" mentioned in this verse is the third day from the time God said these words. Since this was said on the fourth day of their arrival at Sinai, the third day mentioned is the sixth day after they arrived at Mount Sinai, which is the day God said the Ten Commandments.

other laws he had taught them at Marah which included the laws of the Sabbath, civil (monetary) laws, and honoring one's parents.[21]

The Fifth Day: Moses Writes and the People Offer Sacrifices.

Exodus 24:4 - 24:8:

24:4: And Moses wrote all the words of the Lord and rose up early in the morning and built an altar at the foot of the mountain and twelve pillars according to the twelve tribes of Israel."

24:5: And he sent the young men of the Children of Israel who brought burnt offerings and sacrificed peace offerings of oxen to the Lord.

24:6: And Moses took half the blood and put it in basins and half of the blood he dashed against the altar.

24:7: And he took the Book of the Covenant and read in the hearing of the people and they said, "All that the Lord has spoken, we will do and obey."

24:8: And Moses took the blood and sprinkled it on the people and said, "Behold, the blood of the covenant which the Lord has made with you in agreement with all these words."

The sixth day: The Ten Commandments.

19:16-17: It was the third day [after sanctifying themselves] in the morning. There was thunder and lightning. A thick cloud was on the mountain and there was an exceedingly loud call of the shofar growing louder and louder. And all the people who were in the camp trembled.

20:1-2: And God spoke all these words, saying: "I am the Lord your God who brought you out of the land of Egypt out of the house of slavery."

And God continued speaking all the words of the Ten Commandments.

---

21. Commentary of Rashi on Exodus 24:3.

The foregoing are the verses in the Book of Exodus that describe the events of the six days from the time the Children of Israel arrived at Mount Sinai until they heard the the words of the Ten Commandments.

Now, let us examine the verses that describe Jethro's arrival at Mount Sinai to see whether he came before or after the Ten Commandments were heard.

Exodus 18:1-16

18:1: Now, Jethro, the priest of Midian, Moses's father in law, heard of all that God had done for Moses and for Israel His people, how the Lord brought Israel out of Egypt.

18:2: And Jethro, Moses's father-in-law took Zipporah the wife of Moses, after he had sent her away.

18:5: And Jethro, Moses's father-in-law, came with his sons and his wife to Moses into the wilderness where he was camped at the mountain of God.

18:6: And he said to Moses, "I am your father-in-law, Jethro. I am coming to you with your wife and her two sons are with her."

18:7: And Moses went out to greet his father-in-law, and he bowed to him and kissed him, and they asked about each other's well-being and they came into the tent.

The Midrash teaches that Jethro was given great honor when he arrived at Mount Sinai.[22] The entire Israelite nation led by Moses and Aaron, Aaron's sons and the seventy elders went out to greet him. And the Shechina was revealed in honor of Jethro.

18:12: And Jethro, Moses's father-in-law brought a burnt-offering and sacrifices to God. And Aaron came with all the elders of Israel to eat bread with Moses's father-in-law before God.

---

22. Mekhilta, Exodus Rabba, Rashi.

18:13: And it was on the next day that Moses sat to judge the people, and the people stood around Moses from the morning until the evening.

18:14: And when Moses' father-in-law saw all that he was doing for the people, he said, "What is this that you are doing for the people? Why are you sitting alone with all the people standing around you from morning to evening?"

18:15: And Moses replied to his father in law, "The people are coming to me to inquire of God."

18:16: "Whenever they have a matter, they come to me and I judge between man and his neighbor, and I teach them the statutes of God and His laws."

At this point, Jethro warned Moses that he will collapse if he alone takes responsibility for this task. He advised him to establish a fully structured court system. Moses himself should be the supreme judge who hears only cases that are too difficult for the lower courts. Moses took his advice and did everything he said.

A careful examination of the verses will show that it would have been impossible for Jethro to come to Sinai on any one of the five days leading up to God saying the Ten Commandments. All five days were filled from dawn to dusk with other activities: setting up the encampments at Mount Sinai, Moses ascending and descending the mountain to act as an intermediary between God and the people, sanctifying the people, teaching the basic laws, building an altar and offering sacrifices upon it.

And, most certainly, the day that *"Moses sat to judge the people, and the people stood around Moses **from the morning until the evening**,"* could not have been one of the first five days. And the Torah tells us that this was the day after Jethro arrived!

The fact is that the earliest date that Jethro could have arrived at Sinai was four months after the Sinai Revelation, on the very day that Moses brought down the second tablets.[23] For it was on the next day that Moses sat and judged the people.[24]

The presumption that Jethro became Jewish at Mount Sinai is based solely on conjecture with no support from evidence, whereas the Torah itself testifies to Jethro becoming the first post-Sinai *Noahide Ger* and the first friend and brother of the Children of Israel, establishing the legacy of the *Ger*.

The people who want to believe that Jethro became a "kosher Jew" do so because they cherish this great man of wisdom and kindness and they want him to be one of theirs. But in truth, Jethro remained a *Noahide Ger* throughout his life. This is further shown by Jethro's words when he asked to leave Sinai and return home. He told Moses, *"I must go to my own land and to my own family (Numbers 10:30),"* indicating that Midian was still his land and the Kenites were still his people.

If all this is true, why is the portion of the Torah that includes the Ten Commandments named after Jethro? The answer is that Jethro, the priest of Midian, remembered to do what Moses and Aaron and the rest of the Jewish people had forgotten. Jethro blessed God for what He had done for the Children of Israel, His people, as it says, *"And Jethro said, 'Blessed be the Lord who has delivered you out of the hand of the Egyptians and out of the hand of Pharaoh, who has delivered the people from under the hand of the Egyptians (Exodus 18:10).'"*

How embarrassing to have forgotten to bless God for liberating them from Egyptian slavery.[25] Jethro redeemed them all by his blessing. And for this, his name is called on the portion of the Torah that includes the Ten Commandments.

---

23. That day is the 10th day of the Hebrew month of Tishrei, which in the following year became Yom Kippur.

24. Exodus 18:13 Rashi on the verse.

25. One could argue that the prophetic Song at the Sea was praising God, but it was not a blessing in the true sense of the word as was said by Jethro.

Jethro's Struggle

Jethro was unique in the history, the first *Ger Toshav* to arise after the giving of the Torah, a second Abraham in that he became the father to all post-Sinai *Gerim*. And like Abraham, his entire being was filled with wisdom and kindness.

Moses praised Jethro by saying, "All my greatness hinges upon my father-in-law, the chieftain of Midian."[26] And the *Midrash* says that Moses was equal in importance to all of Israel.[27] By inference, this tells us that the greatness of Israel hinges upon its relationship to Jethro.

We saw Jethro run the gamut of spiritual ascent. He began with the rank of *acum* as chief advisor to Pharaoh and High Priest of Midian. From there he became a *nochri*, renouncing the idolatry of Midian and searching for truth, as it says[28], *"He had full knowledge of every idol in the world and left no idol unworshipped."*

Upon arriving at Mount Sinai, he attained the enlightenment of a *Noahide Ger* when he said *"Now I know that the Lord is greater than all the gods (Exodus 18:11)."*

And finally, standing under the wings of the *Shechina* and immersed in Torah among the Children of Israel, Jethro ascended to a level comparable to Aaron the High Priest.

At that point, Jethro had to struggle with the most important decision of his life, a struggle that would become a legacy for every *Noahide Ger* who would come after him. Jethro had to decide whether to remain a *Noahide* or convert and become an Israelite, a Jew.

Moses had said to him, *"We are journeying to the place of which the Lord said, 'I will give it to you.' Come with us and we will shower you with goodness, for the Lord has spoken good concerning Israel (Numbers 10:29)."*

Jethro contemplated Moses's offer of goodness. What could they possibly bestow upon a man of his advanced years?

---

26. Rashi on Exodus 4:18 quoting the Mechilta.

27. Ibid.

28. Mechilta on Exodus 18:11.

Go and calculate the age of Jethro. His wisdom had earned him a position as one of Pharaoh's chief advisors. And it is written, *"A man of fifty offers counsel."*[29] He had fled from Pharaoh before the Egyptians began drowning the Israelite infants in the Nile, which means he left Egypt before Moses was born. Moses was eighty years old when he stood before Pharaoh to liberate the Hebrew slaves. That would make Jethro at least 130 years old when he came to Mount Sinai.

"What goodness can they give me? I have no use for material riches. I have seen honor and ultimately it means nothing. But as an Israelite, I would bask in the light of the *Shechina*. I would receive an exalted new soul that would certainly benefit me in the Eternal World. On the other hand, if I do not return to my kinsmen in Midian to teach them faith in the God of Israel, they will be lost in darkness and impurity forever."

Jethro had to make the choice between good and very good. It is written (Genesis 1:31), *"And God saw all that He had made and, behold, it was very good."* Until that verse, the Torah's account of creation indicates that everything God saw, all His handiwork, was good. Now, at the very end, God saw that it was very good. The difference between good and very good is that very good includes evil. Since this verse comes to include the entire creation, there is evil in it.[30] But He calls it "very good" since the evil is also good, for it includes the evil inclination in man and the dispensation of punishment. Even these are good, as King Solomon wrote, *"To everything there is a season and time for every purpose under the heaven (Ecclesiastes 3:1)."* And the fact is that evil is needed for the preservation of good, for if it were not for the evil inclination, no man would build a house or have children. And if there were no punishment, mankind would have little desire to improve its ways.

Remaining with Moses and becoming a Jew would have been good. But Jethro saw his return to Midian and to his family as very good. It included evil because Midian was a place of great evil and if he failed to teach his family faith in God, he would have lost everything.

---

29. Chapters of the Fathers 5:25.

30. *Ramban* (Rabbi Moses ben Nachman, 1194-1270), the great legal authority and Kabbalist.

In the end, Jethro realized that if he stayed with Moses and became a Jew, he would primarily be serving himself, but if he returned to his family, he would be serving God. And so he said to Moses, "*No, I will not go [with you], rather I must go to my land and my kinsmen (Numbers 10:30)."*

By taking this course of action, Jethro transcended his nature and bonded with the Lord, the God of Israel. This came to Jethro only through self-sacrifice (*mesirat nefesh*) in the service of God. Above this, there is no higher level as long as the soul is in the body.

Had Jethro become a Jew and returned to Midian to convert his family, he would have been going against a *halachic*-based tradition that strongly discourages Jews from proselytizing. Equally significant, he would have failed, for his people, the Kenites, did not become Jews.

But Jethro did not fail. He left Mount Sinai and returned to Midian as a *Noahide Ger* where he inspired the Kenites to become the first nation, besides Israel, to embrace the Noahide Code and settle in the Holy Land as *Gerim Toshavim*, distinguishing themselves as scribes, Torah scholars and good neighbors in Israel.

Note: The *Ohr HaChaim* gives us a different explanation why Jethro was given the honor to have his name on a portion of the Torah. *He writes:*

Ohr HaChaim on Exodus 18:21

God could have found many other ways of compensating Jethro for his good deeds. But I believe the reason for all this is that God wanted to show the Jewish people already at that time and for all future generations that there are great and intelligent men to be found among the nations of the world. Jethro was an example of an enlightened Gentile who demonstrated this beyond question. It is to teach us that if God chose the Jewish people as His people this is not because they possess superior intellectual qualities. God chose the Jewish people as a reward for the loyalty the Patriarchs had shown Him and as an act of love towards this people.

The parable of the breach birth: There is a point of Torah law that says if a mother is in labor and it is a breach birth, and the arm of the infant comes out first, we are permitted to cut off the arm of the baby to save the mother. But if the head of the baby comes out first, then we cannot cut off the head to save the mother. This *halacha* is applied to Jethro. Jethro is the arm of the baby. The Rabbis of an earlier era saw that if Jethro were to be acknowledged as a righteous Gentile, it would endanger the life of Israel, who was like a mother giving birth. Therefore, they cut off the arm by making Jethro a Jew.

As a Jew, Jethro means nothing to the nations of the world, just another old Jew. But as a Gentile, he is the perfect sage filled with wisdom and the spirit of God. And he could have surely inspired a large segment of the world to approach the Torah as *Noahide Gerim*. But this would have brought the wrath of the Church upon the defenseless Jewish communities living in exile in foreign lands. So, they cut off the arm to save the mother. But now, at the beginning of the era of the Final Redemption, the head of Jethro has emerged first and it cannot be cut off to save the mother, who this time is not Israel, but Judaism, the religion of Israel. This is what we call the birth pangs of Messiah.

"And Moses said to Jethro, 'Please do not leave us, for you know our encampments in the wilderness, and you are our eyes. If you come with us, the good that the Divine does for us, you will receive as well (Numbers 10:31,32).'"

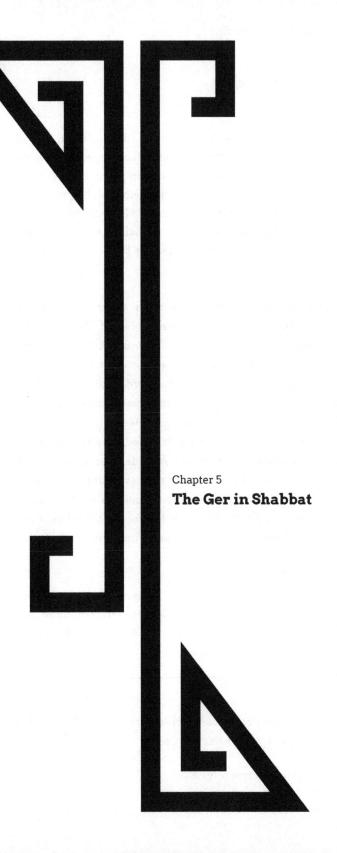

Chapter 5
The Ger in Shabbat

Part One: Permission to Rest

Isaiah 56:6,7

And the B'nei Nechar[1] (Gentiles) who escort the Lord to serve Him and to love the Name of the Lord, to be His servants, everyone who safeguards Shabbat from profaning it and who holds fast to My covenant. I will bring them to My holy mountain and I will cause them to rejoice in My House of Prayer; their burnt offerings and their sacrifices shall be acceptable upon My altar, for My House shall be called a House of Prayer for all peoples.

Resting on the Sabbath is the most venerable of all religious observances. The Jewish people have observed 182,000 consecutive Sabbaths since they crossed the Red Sea nearly 3500 years ago. But the Noahide's heritage of the Sabbath precedes even that of the Jewish people, for the Patriarchs and the sons of Jacob, according to *halacha* (Jewish Law) were Noahides. And it says concerning the Sabbath, *"Abraham would rejoice, Isaac would exult, Jacob and his children would rest on it."*[2]

As was mentioned in the chapter called, Torah of Shem, Abraham observed the *mitzvot* of the Torah hundreds of years before they were given on Mount Sinai.[3] But except for the Seven Universal Laws and the *mitzvah* of circumcision, he observed the commandments through free will and choice, not out of obligation. But for the Children of Israel as a whole, the actual *mitzvot* were not revealed until the Exodus from Egypt.

Exodus 15:22,23

And Moses led Israel onward from the Red Sea and they went into the wilderness of Shur, and they traveled three days in the wilderness and found no water. And when they came to

---

1. The *Ben Nechar* or *Nochri* is a Gentile who no longer believes in idolatry, but has not fully accepted the Noahide Code.

2. Sabbath afternoon prayer service.

3. Babylonian Talmud, Yoma 28b.

Marah, they could not drink the waters of Marah for they were bitter.

Marah was the first encampment of the Israelites after crossing the Red Sea. The Talmud[4] tells us that at Marah the people were given ten *mitzvot*: seven that the Noahides had accepted upon themselves, and three that Moses added: civil laws, the Sabbath, and honoring father and mother.

It is significant that the Shabbat laws were first given at Marah, five and a half weeks before the Children of Israel reached Mount Sinai. This means that when the people were commanded to observe the Sabbath they still had the status of Noahides.[5]

Some commentaries maintain that at Marah they were merely taught the Sabbath laws, but were not yet commanded to keep them. The actual commandment came a few days later when they arrived at the wilderness of Sin, which is between Elim and Sinai.[6]

The day after they arrived in the wilderness of Sin, manna fell from heaven.

Exodus 16:21 - 23

And they gathered it morning by morning, every man according to his eating. And it came to pass on the sixth day [of the week] they gathered twice as much and Moses said: Tomorrow is a rest day, a holy Sabbath unto the Lord. Bake that which you will bake and boil that which you will boil and all that is left over shall be kept until the morning.

---

4. Babylonian Talmud, Sanhedrin 56b.

5. The Israelites were bound only by the Noahide Laws until the giving of the Ten Commandments on Mount Sinai fifty days after the Exodus from Egypt.

6. Exodus 16:1.

This was the first injunction against working on the Sabbath Day, for both baking and cooking are work activities that are forbidden on Shabbat.[7] The people were also forbidden to gather manna on Shabbat, since gathering produce from the ground is also forbidden work. Immediately following these directives, the verse says, *"And the people rested on the seventh day."*[8]

It does not say that the Children of Israel rested on the seventh day, but the people rested, to include the Noahides who had departed from Egypt with Israel.

One might argue that those Noahides were in a special category because they were on their way to Mount Sinai and were soon going to become Jews. And, therefore, they were permitted to keep the Sabbath. But it is a Torah principle that nothing is given in potential unless it is specifically stated as such, as with, *"When you come into the land you will observe...etc."* According to the Torah, every person is judged as he stands at the moment of judgment and future actions for good or bad are not weighed into the balance. Moreover, at Sinai the people were free to accept or reject the Torah, so one could not have predicted with certainty that the Noahides in the wilderness of Sin were going to become Israelites at Mount Sinai.

On Mount Sinai, when God spoke all the words of the Ten Commandments, He specifically mentioned the Noahide in relation to Shabbat:

Exodus 20:8 - 10

Remember the Sabbath day to keep it holy. Six days you shall do all your work. But the seventh day is a Sabbath unto the Lord your God. In it you shall do no manner of work, you, your son, your daughter, your manservant, your maidservant, your

---

7. *Melacha* or "work" that is forbidden on Shabbat is not dependent on exertion, but relates to 39 specific creative activities that were needed to construct the Tabernacle at Mount Sinai. Baking and cooking (in liquid), for example, were needed to produce the dyes for the Tabernacle tapestries and, some say, to bake the Showbread and cook specific sacrifices.

8. Exodus 16:30.

animal, and the **Ger within your gates**. For in six days the Lord
made the heavens and the earth, the sea and all that is in them
and rested on the seventh day. Therefore, the Lord blessed the
Sabbath day and made it holy.

Some Rabbis held the opinion that the **Ger within your gates** refers
to a Jewish convert. But the *Ramban* establishes it unconditionally as
a *Ger Toshav*, a Noahide who has rejected idolatry and has taken on the
Seven Universal Laws. The *Ramban* bases this ruling on another verse
(Deuteronomy 14:21), *"You shall not eat from anything that dies of itself.
You may give it to the **Ger within your gates** so that he may eat it or you
can sell it to a Nochri."*

Obviously, it is forbidden to give non-kosher meat to a Jewish convert,
whose obligations are the same as other Jews and is forbidden to eat such
meat. Therefore, this *Ger* in your gates must be a *Noahide Ger*. From here,
the *Ramban* established every reference to the **Ger within your gates** in
the Torah as a *Noahide Ger*, including this one in the Ten Commandments.

Now that we know that the **Ger within your gates** is not a Jewish
convert, but a Noahide, we can establish his relationship to the Sabbath.

With respect to Shabbat observance, there are two basic categories of
Gentiles and two categories of observance

The two categories of Gentiles are the *Acum* and the *Ger Toshav*.

The *Acum* is an idolater and is forbidden to observe the Sabbath
in any way. He is even forbidden to rest on a weekday as if it were the
Sabbath. And he may not say, "Shabbat shalom," or "Good Shabbos," as a
greeting. Anything the *Acum* does with respect to Sabbath observance is a
desecration of the Sabbath and a desecration of God's Name. We find this
stated explicitly in the *Mishneh Torah* of the *Rambam*,⁹ *"An Acum who
rests even on a weekday, observing that day as a Sabbath, is liable for
the death penalty."*

By contrast, the *Ger Toshav* has the freedom to observe the Sabbath
any way he desires so long as he conforms to *halacha*. Under certain
circumstances he is actually obliged to observe Shabbat like a Jew, as *Rashi*

---

9. *Mishneh Torah*, Laws of Kings 10:10.

writes,[10] *"The Ger Toshav who has taken upon himself not to serve idols but retains the right to eat non-kosher meat is warned by Scripture that his working on the Sabbath it is tantamount to worshipping idols."*

The *Ger Toshav* must refrain from working on the Sabbath when he lives among Jews or works for a Jew, for then he is a **Ger within your gates**. This *Ger Toshav* is forbidden to work on Shabbat because if he does, Jews will learn from him and this will compromise the sanctity of the day. The Jewish people will see him going to the beach or lighting his barbeque and they will say, "If he does it, then we should be able to do it, too."

But when the *Ger Toshav* lives apart from the Jewish community or is not employed by a Jew, he is free to observe Shabbat as his heart moves him. There is a separate verse that guarantees him this right, as it says (Exodus 23:12), *"Six days you shall do your activities and on the seventh day you shall rest so that your ox and your donkey may rest and the son of your maidservant and **the Ger** may be refreshed."* Here, the Ger is not called **in your gates** as in the Ten Commandments, but simply **the Ger**.[11] In this verse, the Torah assures the *Ger Toshav* of his right to rest and be refreshed on Shabbat, but it does not obligate him to refrain from *melacha* (work).

What about the much-quoted view that forbids all Gentiles, regardless of status, from resting on the Sabbath? This opinion clearly contradicts the Talmud which rules that a *Ger Toshav* must cease working on Shabbat, albeit taking a lenient view of the matter. According to this section of the Talmud:[12] A *Ger Toshav* is **permitted** to work for himself on Shabbat in the same manner that an Israelite is permitted to work on the intermediate days of the festivals.[13] Rabbi Akiba says he may work on Shabbat in the

---

10. Babylonian Talmud, Yebamot 48b, Rashi's commentary.

11. Rashi, following the Babylonian Talmud, Yebamot 48b, identifies this *Ger* as the *Ger Toshav*.

12. Babylonian Talmud, Keritot 9a.

13. During the week-long Festivals of Passover and Sukkot, there are intermediate days during which restrictions against work are relaxed compared to the first and last days of the festivals.

same manner as an Israelite on the festival day itself.[14] Rabbi Jose says that a Ger Toshav may do work for himself on the Sabbath in the same manner as an Israelite on a week-day.[15]

By this discussion, we can see that the Ger Toshav is expected to rest in some manner on the Sabbath and the parameters are delineated in the Talmud.

The disagreement among Rabbis over a Gentile's right to rest on the Sabbath can be understood by Rashi's classic commentary on Shema Yisrael, the foundation of Jewish faith:

"Hear O Israel, the Lord our God, the Lord is One (Deuteronomy 6:4)."

Rashi's commentary[16]

Today, the Lord is our God and not the God of the other nations. But in the future He will be One God, as it is stated (Zephaniah 3:9), "for then I will turn to the people a pure speech that they may all call upon the Name of the Lord," and it is stated (Zechariah 14:9), "On that day shall the Lord be One and His Name One."

The Rabbis who forbid all Gentiles the right to observe Shabbat are focused on the Gentiles of earlier generations,[17] all of whom were classified as Acum with no share in the God of Israel. This is in contrast to the Rabbis who focus on the righteous Gentiles of the present day (and the future), acknowledging their right to observe the Sabbath. Today, there are

---

14. This is a stricter view. On the intermediate days of a festival many types of work are permitted, but on the festival day itself, the only work permitted is that which is done to prepare food for the day itself, which includes carrying objects in the public thoroughfare.

15. This is the most lenient opinion. Rabbi Jose permits any and all work activities, but leaves the choice up to the Ger Toshav himself.

16. Rashi, the acronym for Rabbi Solomon ben Isaac, lived from 1040-1105.

17. Rashi lived from 1040-1105, two generations before the Rambam (1138-1204).

tens of thousands of Noahides who call upon the Name of the Lord and are bringing the world closer to the Kingdom of God.

In recent years, *batei din* (rabbinic courts of law) in Jerusalem, the United States, the Netherlands, Australia and elsewhere are conferring the status of *Ger Toshav* upon all Noahides who seek it. The status of *Ger Toshav* today is largely ceremonial, but it distinguishes him from the *Acum* and acknowledges his right to observe all relevant *mitzvot* of the Torah, including the Sabbath.

It is written in Rabbi Moshe Weiner's *Sefer Sheva Mitzvot Hashem:*[18]

> At this time, while we do not accept *Gerim Toshavim* for the sake of granting the privileges [for example, living in the Land of Israel], nevertheless, if he comes before a rabbinical court of three of his own free will to accept upon himself to be a *Ger Toshav*, one of the *Hasidei Umot HaOlam* (Pious Among the Nations), for the sake of accepting his *mitzvoth*, we accept him.

Part Two: The Glory of Shabbat

"This is my God and I will glorify Him, my father's God and I will exalt Him (from the Song at the Sea, Exodus 15:2)."

The Talmud asks,[19] *"How is it possible for man to glorify his Creator? Abba Shaul said: By emulating Him! Just as God is gracious and merciful, so should you be gracious and merciful."*

And just as God rested on the seventh day so should you rest on the seventh day.

A *Ger* can say, *"This is my God and I will glorify Him,"* but can a *Ger* say: *"my father's God and I will exalt Him?"* Perhaps the *Ger's* father

---

18. Sefer Sheva Mitzvot Hashem, page 18. The original Hebrew text reads:

לכן בזמן הזה, אע"פ שאין מקבלין ג"ת לענין זכויותיו ישראל מ"מ אם בא לקבל על עצמו מרצונו להיות גר תושב וחסיד אומ"ה בפני ג', לענין קבלת מצוותיו מקבלין אותו

19. Jerusalem Talmud, Peah 3a.

worshipped another god or no god at all. But since Abraham is the father of all *Gerim*, every *Ger* can say, *"My father's God and I will exalt Him."*

Abraham glorified God by rejoicing on the Sabbath, so it is fitting that his children should glorify God by rejoicing on the Sabbath. In the Kingdom of God, everyone rests on the Seventh Day.

Much debate has been heard about a Noahide's right to be Sabbath observant. But what has been little heard is the essential question: *Why should a Noahide **want** to keep Shabbat?*

What are the benefits of Sabbath observance for the non-Jew? We know that he will be rewarded in the Eternal World to Come for every *mitzvah* he does, but what does Sabbath observance give him in this world now?

Exodus 20:11

In six days, the Lord made heaven and earth the sea and all that is in them and rested on the seventh day, wherefore the Lord blessed the Sabbath day and made it holy.

By observing the Sabbath we are testifying to our belief that God created the world in six days and rested on the seventh. And by so doing, we are included in the blessings and holiness of the Sabbath. As God is eternal, His blessings and bestowals of holiness are eternal.

The concept of eternity is beyond the scope of human intellect, but God has endowed us with the ability to understand His eternal salvation in relation to our own existence. Meditating on the awesome concept of God's eternal blessing brings revelations of truth. Any good thought about God is true.

Eternity means never ending. It also means without beginning (*Ain Techila*), a concept the human mind cannot grasp at all, because there is nothing to which it can be compared. Shabbat is the interface between temporal and eternal. It is the perfection of time.

Every false god had a beginning and will have an end. The God of Israel had no beginning. He always was, is, and will be. That should be the most comforting of all possible thoughts, and the most frightening.

Exodus 31:17

In six days the Lord made heaven and earth and on the seventh day He rested and was refreshed.

The Hebrew word in this verse for "refreshed" is *nafash*, spelled the same as the Hebrew word for soul, *nefesh*. The sages ask,[20] "Did God become tired and needed to rest and be refreshed? No, by resting on the seventh day, God gave the creation a soul, a *nefesh*. *Nafash* is the *nefesh* of creation, the World Soul. One who rests on the Sabbath receives a share of this soul, an additional spiritual component in his life."[21] This added soul is the person's share of the Godly *nafash*.

Deuteronomy 5:15

And you shall remember that you were a slave in the land of Egypt and the Lord your God brought you out from there with a mighty hand and an outstretched arm. Therefore, the Lord your God commanded you to keep the Sabbath day.

When Moses repeated the words of the Ten Commandments in Deuteronomy 5:6-17, he explained why God gave us the Sabbath. The reason is freedom. The Sabbath liberates all who observe it. It is the ultimate liberation. A slave works every day of his life. He lacks the freedom to enjoy a rest day. When the Israelites were slaves of Pharaoh in Egypt, they would have been killed if they stopped working for one day a week. Even mentioning such an idea would have brought them merciless beatings. But God took them out of Egypt and delivered them from the house of bondage. To remember this, He gave us the Sabbath as a perpetual reminder of this freedom.

As a complete day of rest, the Sabbath bestows total freedom which only God has the power to give.[22] Even the souls that are being punished in *gehinnom* (purgatory) are given a reprieve for the entire day of Shabbat.

---

20. *Ramban's* commentary to Exodus 31:17.

21. *Ramban* on Exodus 31:17.

22. Freedom that comes as a result of human agency is imaginary and full of contradictions. From a cosmic perspective, sitting in a deck chair on a beach in the South Pacific is not freedom. Neither is looking into a cell phone and saying, "Mirror, mirror, on the wall. Who is the fairest one of all?"

During the six days of the week, spiritually impure forces (*kelipot/husks*) attach themselves to holiness and divert the flow of Divine energy to themselves, keeping the world locked in darkness. But on the Shabbat, the holy life force of the creation is elevated out of reach and liberated from these *kelipot*.[23] This is why on the Sabbath, we are encouraged to indulge ourselves in food and drink and marital relations.[24] Whatever spiritual damage these indulgences might cause during the six days of the week is nullified on the seventh day. This is a great secret.

Shabbat is a safe harbor in the midst of the raging Floodwaters of Noah, which the Sages teach is the struggle to make a living and thrive in a world filled with tests and challenges, strife and pitfalls, and man's inhumanity towards man. And so the proverb goes, "More than the Jew has kept the Shabbat, the Shabbat has kept the Jew." It will do the same for the Ger. It will do the same for the whole world.

Part Three: Remember and Observe

Remember and observe are the two modes of Sabbath observance.[25] The Hebrew word for remember is *zachor*. The Hebrew word for observe is *shamor*.

"Remembering" refers to honoring and enjoying, or taking delight in the Sabbath day. "Observing" refers to refraining from work. In this context, work does not mean physical exertion. It means the 39 creative work activities (*melachot*) that were used to build the Tabernacle in the desert. These include plowing earth, planting, harvesting, binding sheaves, threshing, winnowing, selecting, grinding, sifting, kneading, baking, shearing wool, washing wool, beating wool, dyeing wool, spinning, weaving, making two loops, weaving two threads, separating two threads, tying, untying, sewing stitches, tearing, trapping, slaughtering, flaying skins, tanning, scraping animal hides, marking animal hides, cutting hides

---

23. *Kitvei Arizal, Sefer Pri Etz Chaim, Sha'ar Shabbat,* chapter one.

24. That does not mean eating forbidden food or getting drunk on alcohol or having illicit sexual relations suddenly becomes kosher. It does not.

25. Exodus 20:8 and Deuteronomy 5:12.

to shape, writing two or more letters, erasing two or more letters, building, demolishing, extinguishing a fire, kindling a fire, final hammer blow, and carrying an object between private and public domains or more than four cubits (2.5 meters) in the public domain.

Since this is a book for and about the *Ger*, we will focus on *zachor* (remember) the Sabbath day, since it is relevant to every *Ger* at all times and in every place.

How do we know that *zachor* (remember) is especially relevant to the *Ger*? One hint comes from the numerical value (*gematria*) of the word *zachor* (*Zayin-Khaf-Vav-Resh*), which is 233, the same *gematria* as *l'Ger*, for the *Ger*.[26]

This is in contrast to *shamor* (observe) which has a *gematria* of 546, the same numerical value as *ha'Yisrael*, the Israelite.

Zachor refers to the things we do to honor the Sabbath day and to enjoy it. This includes the weekday preparations for Shabbat that help us remember the Sabbath all week long. For example, if you are in a market and see an especially nice cut of meat or piece of fruit or other tasty treat, you can purchase it and set it aside for the Sabbath. Or, when buying a new article of clothing, you can wait until Shabbat to wear it for the first time. Or, Friday morning can become the scheduled time to change the bed linens, so that you can enjoy the luxury of newly laundered sheets when you slide into bed Friday night.

None of these are practices are hard and fast rules, but they all play their part in honoring the Sabbath and are aspects of *zachor*. These are not obligations, but opportunities.

Friday is *Erev Shabbat*.[27] The entire day is a transition from the mundane to the holy, not always an easy leap. Unless there is a time restraint because of career or school, much of every Friday is normally spent in Shabbat preparations.

Imagine hearing that a great Queen was coming to spend a day in your house as a guest. Would you not make certain that everything is spotlessly

---

26. The letters of the Hebrew alphabet are also numbers. *Alef* is one, *Beth* is two, *Gimel* is three, etc. To derive meaning from the numerical value of Hebrew words is called *gematria*.

27. Thursday night is included in Friday.

clean and orderly? The Talmudic sages viewed the Sabbath as just that, a Queen, the *Shechina*.

Rabbi Hanina put on his finest robes and at sunset Friday evening exclaimed, "Come and let us go forth to welcome the Sabbath Queen." Rabbi Jannai dressed in his best garments and sang, "Come, O bride, Come, O bride!"[28]

Whether it is winter when the days are short or summer when they are long, Fridays seem too brief to get everything done on time. The floors need to be vacuumed or swept and mopped, particularly the floors in the kitchen, the dining room and the bathrooms. Freshly cut flowers are arranged on the dining room table or nearby.[29] Haircuts are taken, fingernails are clipped, shoes are shined, and everyone has either taken a bath or a shower or immersed in a *mikvah*. *Challah*, the traditional Sabbath loaves, is baked or bought, placed on the table and covered with a traditional white satin cloth.

The candles are prepared for lighting and the table is set with the best crystal, china and silverware, or at least a higher grade of disposable plasticware. Families that refrain from *melacha* on Shabbat make sure that the food for the seventh day is cooked on Friday and set on a warming plate before sunset.

Erev Shabbat may become hectic and tempers sometimes flare as sunset approaches, but it is always a day of joy and accomplishment. Perhaps most important of all, time is taken to prepare oneself mentally and emotionally for the peace and joy and freedom of Shabbat. This is accomplished by taking some time out to quietly learn through the weekly Torah portion, all of it or some of it, which is called "living with the times."

Many people listen to music Friday afternoon to bring a taste of Shabbat into the home. There is a wide liturgy of classic Shabbat table songs and hymns and most of it can be found on the internet. And the *Erev Shabbat* mood music does not have to be Jewish. It can be pure and simple folk music from Irish to Japanese to sitar and tabla. Nothing prepares the

28. Babylonian Talmud, Shabbat 119a.

29. Some Kabbalists teach that cut flowers are not a positive thing and do not belong in the home. Live flowers are much preferred.

house for Shabbat more than the right kind of mood music playing in the background Friday afternoon.

It is the way of holiness to treat Shabbat as a touchstone for the rest of the days of the week. Sunday, Monday and Tuesday are connected to the previous Shabbat. On Wednesday, we turn the corner and begin heading for coming Shabbat. By Thursday and Friday, the taste of Shabbat is definitely in the air. In Hebrew, the days of the week are explicitly connected to Shabbat.[30] Sunday is called the First Day of Shabbat, Monday is the Second Day of Shabbat, and so forth. In fact, the word for "week" in Hebrew is Shabbat.[31]

The *Arizal* taught that a proper arrangement of the week is to utilize Sundays and Fridays for meditation since both days are connected to Shabbat. Mondays and Thursdays are for Torah study. Tuesdays and Wednesdays are for financial pursuits. And Saturday is Shabbat, the holy day of rest.

An example of the honor (*kavod*) that is given to Shabbat is expressed by how people greet each other. On Shabbat they do not say, "Good morning." They say, "Good Shabbos" or "Shabbat shalom." They do not say, "Good afternoon. They say, "Good Shabbos" or "Shabbat shalom." They do not say, "Hello" or "Goodbye." They say, "Good Shabbos" or "Shabbat shalom." All greetings or farewells on this day are the same, either good Shabbos or Shabbat shalom. This is in fulfillment of the words of the Prophet Isaiah:

Isaiah 58:13,14
If you restrain your feet because of the Sabbath, refrain from tending to your own needs on My holy day; if you proclaim the Sabbath "a delight," the holy [day] of the Lord, honored for the holiness of the Lord, and you honor it by not doing your own ways, and from seeking your needs and speaking inappropriate words. Then you will be joyous with the Lord and I shall cause you to ride upon the heights of the world, and feed you with the

---

30. These familiar names of the weekdays, Sunday, Monday, Tuesday, etc., are derived from the names of false gods whose rulership ostensibly dominated each respective day. Wednesday is Wotan's day. Thursday is Thor's day, etc.

31. The more commonly used Hebrew word for a week is *shavua*.

heritage of your forefather Jacob, for the mouth of the Lord has
spoken.

For the *Ger* this simply means that all the blessings of Shabbat
become his heritage when he looks to Jacob as his forefather, as it says,[32]
*"And in you [Jacob] and in your seed shall all the families of the world
be blessed."* And the *Rashbam*[33] employs an alternative meaning of the
Hebrew word, "blessed," as "grafted," interpreting the verse to mean that
all the families of the earth shall be grafted into the Congregation of Jacob.

This also suggests that the *Noahide Ger* is entitled to learn *"Col
HaTorah Culah,"* every aspect of the Torah, not merely the Seven Laws of
Noah, as it says (Deuteronomy 33:4), *"The Torah that Moses commanded
us is the heritage of the Congregation of Jacob."*

Kindling the Sabbath lights

The mother of all *Gerim* is Sarah, the wife of Abraham. Abraham
and Sara brought hundreds of souls under the sheltering wings of the
Shechina. Abraham converted the men and Sara converted the women.[34]
The verb for "convert" is *m'gayer* in the masculine and *m'gayeret* in the
feminine.

Today, these terms are used exclusively with reference to conversion
to Judaism, but in the generation of Abraham and Sara there was no
concept as conversion to Judaism because the Torah had not yet been
given.[35] To Abraham and Sara making *Gerim* meant bringing people to the
true faith in God. The foundation of this faith was observance of the Seven
Laws of Noah.

---

32. Genesis 28:14.

33. Rabbi Samuel ben Meir (1085-1158), one of the leading Torah scholars of
his generation in France.

34. Genesis 12:5, *Rashi* on the verse.

35. Abraham was born in the Hebrew year 1948, exactly 500 years before the
Torah was given on Mount Sinai.

Sarah was the first woman to light a lamp on Friday afternoon in honor of the Sabbath. Sara's light illuminated her tent through the Sabbath and continued burning until the next Friday afternoon when she would clean them and light them again.[36]

Sara lit with olive oil rather than candles. There are women today who continue the tradition of lighting with olive oil even though it is costly and more difficult to manage. But candles are the norm.

Some women use tall white candles. Others use tea candles. And some make a point of using beeswax candles imported from Israel.

Shabbat candlesticks in Jewish homes are handed down from mother to daughter or from mother to daughter-in-law for many generations. If it had not been for persecutions and confiscation of Jewish property during the long exile, there would be candlesticks or oil lamps in families dating back a thousand years and more.

When Sarah died, Isaac grieved for the loss of his mother until he married Rebecca and brought her into his mother's tent whereupon she lit the Shabbat lamp, as it says, *"And Isaac was comforted after his mother's death."*[37]

The word for "comforted" in this verse is *"nachem."* It is the same word used to indicate "rest" on Shabbat and the same root word as the name Noah (*Noach* in Hebrew).

Lighting Shabbat candles is as comforting today as it was when it illuminated Sarah's tent nearly four thousand years ago. It is the "shalom" of Shabbat shalom, for the Sabbath lights spread peace throughout every home in which they are lit.

The customary time for lighting is eighteen minutes before sundown. The candles are not lit after sundown and certainly not after nightfall because it is written in the Torah, *"You shall not kindle a fire in any of your dwellings on the Sabbath day."*[38] As with all observances, *Noahide Gerim* are expected to act in accord with *halacha.*

---

36. Genesis Rabba 60.

37. Genesis 24:67.

38. Exodus 35:3.

Some women light two candles. Others light a candle for each member of the family. The candles are generally white and never red, since the color red is symbolic of strict judgment, and on the Sabbath judgment is suspended and mercy prevails in all the worlds.

Lighting the Sabbath candles is an auspicious time for the woman of the house to offer words of gratitude to God for the blessings He has bestowed upon her and to pray for the welfare of her family and friends. It is also customary to put a few coins in a charity box just before lighting.

In many homes, the man of the house will light the candles ahead of time and extinguish them. This singes the wicks and makes them easier to light. His participation also gives him a share in the lighting. And it is his job to gently remind his wife when the time to light the candles has arrived.

As she prepares to light, she meditates on having been chosen as a messenger of God who has given her the strength to dispel darkness by lighting the Sabbath lights of peace. Upon lighting, she recites the blessing, "Blessed are you O Lord our God, Who blesses and sanctifies the Sabbath."

After she has kindled the lights and finished saying her prayers, she meditates on the light that now appears before her eyes. Although there are two or more candles with two or more flames, there is only one light emanating from them. This is the secret of Oneness.

Blessing children

It is customary for a father to bless his children before the Friday night meal. He places both hands on his sons' heads and blesses them one at a time by saying, "May you become as Abraham," and then, "May the Lord bless you and keep you. May the Lord shine His face towards you and be gracious to you. May the Lord turn His countenance to you and grant you peace."[39]

In a similar manner, he blesses each of his daughters by saying, "May the Lord make you as Sarah," followed by the benediction, "May the Lord bless you and keep you, etc."

---

39. Numbers 6:24-26.

Kiddush (Sanctification)

The word *zachor* is from the same Hebrew root word as *l'hazkir*, to mention. Mentioning the sanctity of Shabbat is the core of remembering it. Through speech we bring concepts and feelings into the world. This finds its fullest expression in saying Kiddush before the Sabbath evening meal over a cup of wine or grape juice.

Kiddush is rabbinic in origin, not Scriptural, but it is the essence of Shabbat holiness, the spiritual mate of lighting Shabbat candles. Just as lighting dispels darkness, *Kiddush* uses wine, which has the power to destroy man, to elevate and sanctify the day.

Any cup will do and any grape wine or grape juice will do, but this is a sacrament deserving of the finest. So, it is fitting that one's *Kiddush* cup is sterling silver[40] or at least silver-plated or fine crystal or any other cup that brings honor to the ceremony. Gold is never used because the vessels of the Holy Temple were gold and the Temple is in ruins; may it be rebuilt soon in our days.

The wine or grape juice used should be certified kosher. It is not because a *Ger* has to drink kosher wine. But the holiness of *Kiddush* warrants the use of kosher wine or grape juice because of their sacramental nature. This, too, is an opportunity not an obligation.

The cup is filled with wine or grape juice and held in the man's right hand. If he is left-handed, his left hand is considered as his right hand. Everyone stands as he recites the following:

From Genesis 1:31, 2:1-3
And there was evening and there was morning the sixth day. And the heavens and earth were finished and all their host. On the seventh day God completed His work which He had done and He rested on the seventh day from all His work which He had done. And God blessed the seventh day and sanctified it

---

40. In truth, a silver cup is ruinous for the taste of wine and wine stored in lead crystal can be dangerous to one's health. But the wine for *Kiddush* is poured into the cup and then almost immediately consumed. And during the meal, one's wine glass (if one drinks wine during the meal) is not the *Kiddush* cup but an ordinary glass goblet.

because on it He rested from all His work which God created and made to function.

One who can read and understand Hebrew may want to say these verses in Hebrew.

After the Biblical verses are recited, the one making *Kiddush* recites two blessings:

Blessed are you, O Lord our God, King of the universe, who creates the fruit of the vine (everyone answers, "Amen").

Blessed are you, O Lord our God Who blesses and sanctifies the Sabbath. (everyone answers, "Amen").

The one making *Kiddush* sits down and drinks the wine or grape juice. He can then add some wine or grape juice from the bottle to refill his cup and pours some from his cup into his wife's cup and into everyone else's cup at the table. Some people choose to pour a little wine or grape juice into everyone's cup before reciting Kiddush, and they all drink when he does.

Lechem Mishneh (Two loaves of bread)

Kiddush is a prelude to the Shabbat evening meal. The ceremonial aspect of the meal itself is the bread that is eaten first. Two loaves rest on a cutting board under a decorative white cloth as a reminder of double portion of manna that appeared on the sixth day (Friday), one portion for that day and a second portion for Shabbat, the next day.

In Jewish homes, the head of household raises the two loaves and recites the blessing, "Blessed are You, O Lord our God, King of the universe, Who brings forth bread from the earth." He then cuts a slice for himself and dips it three times in salt that was either sprinkled on the cutting board or sits in a nearby salt dish, and takes a bite of the bread.[41] Then he cuts slices for everyone at the table, dipping each slice three times in salt and handing them out, first to his wife, and then to everyone else at the

---

41. The reason he eats before handing out bread to others is because there should be no pause between saying the blessing and eating the bread.

table. Dipping in salt is a reminder of the Holy Temple, where the offerings upon the Altar were dipped in "a covenant of salt."[42]

The two loaves of bread are called *challah* after the dough portion given to Jewish priests (*Kohanim*) during times of the Temple. The classic Jewish *challah* is a rich egg bread, usually a loaf made from three braids. In recent years, a widespread move towards healthier eating has inspired young women to experiment with whole wheat, rye and spelt flour for baking *challah*. But the old guard rail against this, claiming that in Europe they knew full well what dark bread was, and they will tell you that on Shabbat, "Everything should be white including the bread!"

After the bread is tasted by all, the meal begins. The *Ger* Shabbat evening meal has no restrictions and may consist of whatever food the people enjoy most. This is *oneg* Shabbat, delighting in the Sabbath. The spiritual power of this meal is so great that one who enjoys it is lifted above any punishment of *gehinnom*[43] he or she may have earned as a punishment during the previous week.[44]

In Jewish homes in the west, a Friday night meal may typically begin with fish, then chicken soup, and as many as twenty-one dishes, including condiments, salads, vegetables, puddings (*kugel*), rice or potatoes, and the main entrée of fowl or red meat or both. And then a dessert consisting of fruit compote or cake, followed by nuts and candies and a hot cup of tea or coffee. Vegetarians have equally elaborate meals, particularly if they eat eggs and cheese and are willing to take the time to make casseroles and quiches, curried dishes, rice and vegetables, salads, pies and cakes.

Many Sabbath observant people eat extremely simple fair during the week and pull out all the stops for Shabbat. It is not uncommon to hear about families that are strict vegetarians all week long, but eat chicken or meat on Shabbat. This was the way of Abraham Isaac Kook, the first Chief

---

42. Numbers 18:19

43. Purgatory.

44. Shulchan Arukh HaRav, Hilchos Shabbos.

Rabbi of Israel.[45] Of course, in the Jewish home everything is kosher. The *Ger* approaches the subject of *kashrut* in whatever manner he chooses. He can keep kosher a little or a lot or not at all. So long as everyone enjoys the Friday night meal, it is a success gastronomically and spiritually.

One of the great things about the Friday night meal is that it is likely to attract all the members of the family, even the grown-up children and bring them to the Shabbat table. Binding the family together in an atmosphere of Sabbath holiness and warmth accompanied by good food and drink is its own reward that pays dividends for generations.

It is meritorious to say words of Torah at the Shabbat meal, a story or perhaps a teaching from the weekly Torah portion. These words are like seeds that are dropped on the hearts of children. One day the children will grow up, their hearts will open, the seeds will drop in and the Tree of Life will grow, as it says, *"If three have eaten at the same table and have spoken words of Torah there, it is as if they have eaten from the table of God."*[46]

Inviting guests to the Shabbat meal

Abraham, the father and chief role model of all *Gerim*, was a very wealthy man who kept his tent open on all four sides as a symbol of the generous hospitality he lavished on everyone. Abraham spent his great fortune on charitable acts of kindness, giving people a place to sleep and food to eat and, if possible, a livelihood. And he taught them the knowledge of God.

To resemble Abraham means having guests on Shabbat, feeding people who need a meal. This does not necessarily mean the poor or homeless though it certainly could include them. The person needing a meal could be a visitor from out of town or a couple who are remodeling their kitchen or someone who wants a break from cooking, or people who simply like your company and want a taste of Shabbat the way you prepare it.

---

45. Rabbi Kook was the Ashkenazi Chief Rabbi from 1921-1935, before Israel became a state.

46. Chapters of the Fathers 3:4.

The guardian angels of the seventy nations are called ministers, *sarim* in Hebrew. Abraham was called a *Nasi Elokim*, a Prince of God,[47] a higher level than the ministering angels. Among the thousands of guests that Abraham hosted and fed were three great angels, spiritual beings who do not eat physical food. But it was the will of God that these angels transcend their nature and actually eat the food that Abraham gave them.[48] Not only are all the families of the earth blessed through Abraham,[49] but he was chosen by God to be a source of sustenance for the angels, all because of his trait of lovingkindness.

One of the delights associated with having guests on Shabbat is walking them part of the way home after the meal. This is more evident in homes where they do not drive their cars on Shabbat. On a summer Friday evening, leisurely walking with your guests after the meal can be one of the highlights of the day. And in the winter, all bundled up and trudging through the snow, you are warmed by the knowledge that escorting your guests on their way is a *mitzvah*, and you have done it with self-sacrifice.[50]

"And Abraham planted an eshel-tree (tamarisk) in Beersheva and there he called upon the name of Lord, the Eternal God (Genesis 21:33)."

Abraham planted the tree of hospitality. The Hebrew word, "*eshel*" is an acrostic for *ochel* (food), *sheina* (lodging) and *livuy* (accompanying), the three essential duties of a host.

Part Three: Rest and Refreshed

It is a duty for every Ger to rest and be refreshed on the Shabbat.[51] How this is accomplished is up to the individual. Some people align themselves with the Jewish community. They eat three festive meals, listen to the

---

47. Genesis 23:5.

48. Ibid., 18:8.

49. Ibid., 12:3.

50. If you are stuffed from the meal and exhausted from a particularly rough week, you are excused.

51. Exodus 23:12.

Torah being read in the synagogue Saturday morning, and go to a study or discussion group in the afternoon. Others get out in nature and go to a park or relax by a lake or stream, or picnic in some quiet spot, or gaze at the wonders of the night sky and contemplate the greatness of the Creator.

Each of the Patriarchs had his own distinctive way of resting and being refreshed on the Shabbat. *"Abraham rejoiced on it, Isaac sang songs on it, Jacob and his children rested on it with a rest of love and giving, a rest of truth and faith, a rest of peace and serenity and tranquility and security, a perfect rest in which God found favor."*[52]

Havdalah Ceremony

On Saturday night, when three medium-sized stars can be seen in the sky, there is a tradition to mark the end of Shabbat with *Havdalah*, a ceremony that acknowledges the distinction between the holy and the secular.

A cup, usually the same cup used for *Kiddush*, is filled with wine or grape juice until it is slightly overflowing, an expression of the verse, *"You have anointed my head with oil, my cup runneth over (Psalms 23:5)."*

A braided *Havdalah* candle with multiple wicks is taken and lit, then held aloft for everyone to see. *Havdalah* candles are sold in all Judaica bookstores. If one does not have a *Havdalah* candle, two candles can be lit and held together so that the two flames become one.

Ground spices, such as cinnamon or cloves, or a blend of fragrant spices are placed on the table in front of the one making *Havdalah*. Fresh aromatic herbs from the garden are excellent for this. Some people use a specially made silver or wooden spice box, but any spice jar will do.

The one saying *Havdalah* raises the cup with his right hand, and says:

God is my salvation, I shall trust and not fear, for God the Lord is my might and my praise and my song and He was a salvation for me. (This is an abbreviated version of the full text which can be found in any Hebrew-English prayer book).

Now he says four blessings:

Blessed are You O Lord our God, King of the universe, Who creates the fruit of the vine (everyone says, "amen").

---

52. Siddur, Shabbat afternoon prayer service.

He does not drink at this time, but sets the cup down, picks up the spice jar and says: Blessed are You O Lord our God, King of the universe, Who creates spices of fragrance (everyone says, "amen"). The one making *Havdalah* smells the spices and passes the jar around for everyone else to smell the fragrance.

The person holding the candle raises it a bit higher and the one making *Havdalah* says: Blessed are You O Lord our God, Who creates the lights of the fire (everyone says, "amen"). Everyone holds up their right hand to see the candlelight reflecting off their fingernails.

Finally, the one making *Havdalah* says: Blessed are You O Lord our God, King of the universe, Who separates between holy and mundane, between light and darkness, between Israel and the nations, between the seventh day and the six days of work. Blessed are You O Lord Who separates between holy and secular (everyone says, "amen").

The one making *Havdalah* sits, lifts the cup and drinks it. He takes the candle from the hand of the one holding it and extinguishes the flame in the overflow wine that is in the bowl.

The custom is to mention the Prophet Elijah and the Messiah in a brief song: Elijah the prophet, Elijah the Tishabite, Elijah the Giladite. May he come soon in our days with the Messiah the son of David.

The *Havdalah* service formally ends the Sabbath with words of praise and honor, just as Kiddush inaugurated it with words of praise and honor.   The reason for smelling the spices is to refresh everyone after the departure of the Shabbat soul, *Nafash*. The candle is lit as a remembrance that God gave the gift of fire to Adam the night following the first Shabbat to illuminate the darkness of the world.

✡ ✡ ✡ ✡

Shabbat is an island in time. Time is its boundary, but Shabbat is not about time. The seventh day begins and ends according to the rotation of the Earth on its own axis in the presence of the Sun. Thus, Shabbat can be measured by movement through space. But Shabbat is not about space or movement. Shabbat is above nature clothed in nature. It is a holy gift from the treasury of God that stands above time and space, but exists within time and space one day every week. Shabbat is a state of being. If you enter it, you experience a taste of the World to Come. *Nafash*.

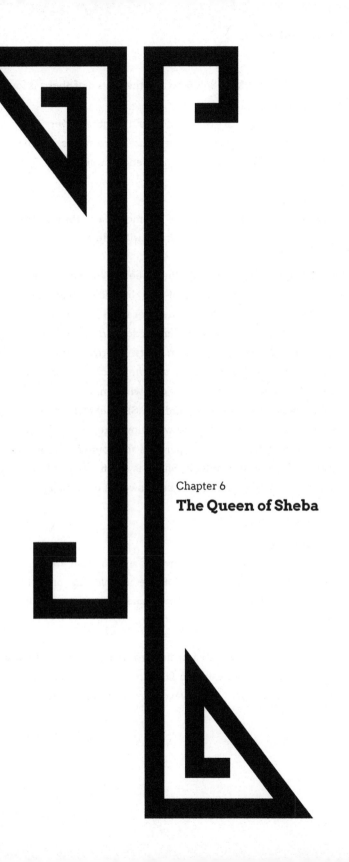

Chapter 6
The Queen of Sheba

The narrative about King Solomon and the Queen of Sheba is found in the First Book of Kings 10:1-13.

On the surface, it appears to be a story of two great sovereigns paying tribute to each other with gold and silver, jewels and spices. But in truth, it is about the soul of a *Noahide Ger* seeking redemption.

Kings 10:1
The Queen of Sheba heard of Solomon's fame through the Name of God, and she came to test him with riddles.

The opening verse tells us that the Queen of Sheba learned of King Solomon's fame through the Name of God. In this context, the Name of God means the revelation that awakened her from her slumber, as it says (Jeremiah 3:14), *"Return wayward children, says the Lord, for I am your husband, and I will take you one from a city and two from a family and bring you to Zion. And I will give you shepherds according to My heart and they will feed you with knowledge and wisdom."*

The Queen of Sheba was husbandless. She heard reports about the Divine wisdom of King Solomon and was moved to see for herself if the reports were true. If they were true, perhaps she could find liberation and enlightenment from him. Suddenly, Sheba is on the way to Jerusalem to test Solomon with riddles that could be answered only by a person with Divine wisdom.

Kings 10:2
And she came to Jerusalem with an enormous treasure, camels bearing spices and a fortune in gold and precious gemstones, and she came to Solomon and spoke to him all that was in her heart.

The Queen of Sheba was an amazing woman, endowed with wisdom and understanding, a rare beauty in face and form, and a monarch who ruled with absolute authority over a vast and wealthy empire that extended from Yemen to Ethiopia and gave her great wealth, gold, diamonds and sapphires, and costly spices.[1]

But the Queen of Sheba was a descendant of Ham, the third son of Noah, and she was an idol worshipper.

Spiritually, her heritage was from Eliezer, the servant of Abraham, also a descendant of Ham.

When Abraham asked Eliezer to go to Haran to find a wife for his son, Isaac, Eliezer asked Abraham why Isaac could not marry his daughter. Abraham answered that he could not give Isaac to Eliezer's daughter because Eliezer, as a descendant of Canaan the son of Ham, had been cursed by Noah (Genesis 9:25), *"Cursed is Canaan, a slave of slaves shall he be to his brothers."*

Since Isaac was to be a primary factor in bringing the world to perfection, he could not mix his bloodline with a bloodline that carried a curse.

The Queen of Sheba wanted to know whether she fell under this curse. It was possible that she was a descendant of Canaan, as it says (Gen. 10:18), *"and the families of Canaan spread abroad."* But she might also have been a descendant of Ham's first born son, Cush, who did not fall under Noah's curse. If Solomon's wisdom was Divine, he could tell her if she was subject to Noah's curse,[2] and if she was, he could tell her how to nullify it. Perhaps he could nullify it himself. So she was aroused by God to test Solomon to see if his wisdom was human or Godly.

Kings 10:3

And Solomon explained to her the depth of meaning of all her words; there was nothing hidden from the king that he did not explain to her.

---

1. Yemen is the world's primary source of frankincense, one of the chief spices of the Temple incense.

2. Cush was the original name of Ethiopia, indicating that its people were descendants of Cush. Since Sheba ruled over Ethiopia, she might have been a descendant of Cush and not Canaan.

Solomon successfully answered all of the Queen of Sheba's riddles and went far beyond that, explaining everything that was in her heart. He read her mind and revealed thoughts to her that she had not yet thought, but would think in the future.

Kings 10:4-6

And the Queen of Sheba saw all the wisdom of Solomon and the house that he had built. And the food of his table and his staff of servants and the level of his ministers and their fine clothing and his drink stewards and the burnt offerings that were sacrificed in the Temple of the Lord, and there was no longer a spirit within her.

The Queen of Sheba was awestruck by the glory of King Solomon's world. As great as her royal court was, it was nothing compared to this Jewish monarchy. The perfection of each detail and the quality of Solomon's staff of servants and ministers dazzled her.

The inner essence of the world is its people.[3] Do not be fooled by beautiful landscapes, by mountains and lakes and magnificent forests. The measure of a place is its people. And in Solomon's court, the Queen of Sheba saw people of brilliance and refinement beyond any she had ever known or imagined. She saw that this was a realm beyond the natural, a kingdom that could have been built only by Divine wisdom.

When she was sufficiently impressed, Solomon took her to the Holy Temple, and brought burnt offerings upon the Great Sacrificial Altar.[4] She saw the archangel Ariel descend from heaven in the form of a fiery lion to consume the sacrifices.[5]

She smelled the sweet aroma of the *ketoret*, the Temple incense, and heard the Levites singing the Psalms of David accompanied by an orchestra of hundreds of musicians playing upon harps, lutes, cornets, flutes, drums and tambourines. Her emotions soared to the heavens. It was as if God had

---

3. Shaar Kavanot of the Arizal.

4. Targum Yonatan.

5. II Chronicles 7:1. Zohar I, 6b; III, 32b, 211a.

taken away her spirit and had given her a new one, as it says (Psalms 51:12), *"Create in me a pure heart, O God, and renew within in me an upright spirit."*

When she learned that Solomon had built this Temple to the Name of the God of Israel, she said to the king:

Kings 10:6-9

"The words I heard in my land about your deeds and your wisdom were true. But I did not believe these things until I came and saw them with my own eyes, and beheld that not even half had been told to me; you have more wisdom and goodness that the report I had heard."

God had brought the Queen of Sheba to Zion. He gave her King Solomon as a shepherd who taught her wisdom and knowledge from the Torah. He revealed to her God's love of the Children of Israel, how He had purified them with harsh bondage in Egypt. And then, He liberated them and carried them to Mount Sinai and gave them the Torah and the mission of teaching the Seven Laws of Noah to the nations of the world.

She listened intently and then asked a question as difficult to answer as her riddles, "No Israelite came to teach us that the sun was not God. No Israelite came to teach us that there was a God Who spoke and the world came into being. Why has Israel failed in its mission?"

Solomon said to her (Song 5:2), *"I am asleep, but my heart is awake."*

All of mankind, even the wisest of men, even Solomon himself is in a hypnotic trance. The hypnotic trance brainwashes people to think that God does not exist. And the people who know that God does exist are taught by the hypnotic trance that you cannot trust Him because He is not really good.

And so, everyone is given something else to trust and love other than God. It can be the sun or the moon or an avatar or a sage or a philosophy or one's own thoughts about what life is all about. These are the false gods of the hypnotic trance. But one day soon the trance will be shattered. The world will learn true faith in God and mankind will begin to trust God. And the *Ger* will lead the way to this Redemption.

The Queen of Sheba said to Solomon:

Kings 10:8,9

"Fortunate are your men, fortunate are the servants who stand before you at all times and hear your wisdom.

"May the Lord your God be blessed Who desired you to place you on the throne of Israel. It was because of the eternal love of the Lord for Israel that He appointed you king to do justice and righteousness."

The Queen of Sheba had renounced her idol worship. She saw that everything in her life had come to her directly from the hand of the Lord and that she could trust him completely.

Every being in creation, from the mightiest angel to the lowliest worm at the bottom of the sea, desires to receive goodness and bestow goodness upon others. But God already has all the goodness and desires to bestow it on whoever will accept it.

The Queen of Sheba had been given a new soul, the soul of a righteous *Noahide Ger*. She accepted the Seven Laws of Noah and was given a share of Eternal life in the World to Come. God loved her and she knew it, and she loved Him for it.

Kings 10:10

And she gave the king one hundred and twenty talents of gold and a great volume of spices and precious gemstones; never again was such an abundance of spices seen as the Queen of Sheba gave to King Solomon.

It was stated at the outset that the Queen of Sheba was rich and powerful, but even among the wealthiest kings and potentates the gifts she presented to Solomon were unprecedented. One hundred and twenty talents does not sound like an exceptional amount of gold, but it is. A talent of gold is 42.5 kilos or 42,500 grams. At the current price (November 2014), the market value of a gram of gold is $42.00. This means that the gold the Queen of Sheba gave Solomon, by today's standards, would be worth approximately two billion dollars. This is besides the treasure in diamonds and sapphires and rare spices that she presented to him.

Kings 10:13

King Solomon gave the Queen of Sheba all her desire that she asked for, aside from what he gave her according to the ability of King Solomon; and she turned around and went to her land, she and her servants.

Sheba had one last question to ask Solomon. It had been the reason she came to see him in the first place. "I am a descendant of Ham, the son of Noah. I want to know if Noah's curse falls on me and my family and my people?"

Solomon answered her definitively, "No, it does not."

"How can you be so certain? Can you trace my bloodline back to its source?"

"If you were the daughter of Canaan or even if you were Canaan himself, Noah's curse would not fall on you."

"I need to understand why not."

Solomon continued, "God appointed seventy angelic princes to oversee the seventy principal nations of man. But there is no angelic prince over Israel, only God Himself. Now that you have become a righteous *Ger* by observing the Seven Laws of Noah, you have been taken out from under the princely overseer of Canaan and have been grafted into Israel. Nothing that applied to Canaan or any of his descendants applies to you any longer. This would not have been the case before Israel received the Torah at Mount Sinai. Had you accepted the Seven Laws of Noah before the revelation at Sinai, you would not have become subject to the supervision of God Himself. But at Mount Sinai the world changed. The Children of Israel became a nation of priests and a holy people and the rest of the world went through a change in potential. Even the ancient Canaanites, whom we were commanded to destroy because of their evil ways, were spared if they accepted the Seven Laws of Noah. Neither you nor any of your descendants nor any of your people who follow the ways of the Torah are subject to Noah's curse."

She asked him, "Can I believe you?"

"I am willing to swear to you that I am telling the truth."

"I want you to do more than that. I want you to prove to me that there is no curse upon my bloodline by fathering a child with me. That is all I desire. That is what I ask."

Solomon said, "I will do what you ask."

Solomon and Sheba slept together and conceived a child.

Soon after that, she returned to her home satisfied that she knew the truth and that it was good. She had been blessed by God.

When the Queen of Sheba arrived in Ethiopia, she led all the people under her dominion to renounce idol worship. The chronicles of Ethiopian history tell us that the people "walked in the ways of the God of Jacob" for the next 1200 years.

The Jewish sages say that a daughter was born to King Solomon and the Queen of Sheba.[6] She became the ancestor of Nebuchadnezzar, the king of Babylon who destroyed the Holy Temple and led the Jews into Babylonian exile.

✡ ✡ ✡ ✡

The people of Ethiopia have an ancient tradition that tells a different version of the story of King Solomon and the Queen of Sheba. It is a legend that forms "the bedrock of Ethiopian national and religious feeling"[7] to this day. The story is completely outside of Jewish tradition. We include it only to show the mindset of a nation whose people adopted Judaism without becoming Jewish.

When she arrives, she is greeted with great ceremony. She presents Solomon with lavish gifts of gold and jewels and rare spices and is amazed by his wisdom and regal bearing. The legend begins when the Queen of Sheba, Ethiopia's reigning monarch at the time, hears that King Solomon was the wisest of all men on earth, so she sets out on a journey to Jerusalem to hear his wisdom.

Solomon tells her that all his wisdom was given to him by the God of Israel, a God that she does not know. She says that her people worship the sun whom they call the creator and king. She admits that no man had ever told them that there is a God greater than the sun.

The Queen says, "From this moment I will not worship the sun, but I will worship the Creator of the sun, the God of Israel. He shall be a

---

6. Midrash Hava b'Shashelet HaKabbalah 42.

7. Edward Ullendorff, The Schweich Lectures, 1967.

God to me and to my seed after me and unto all the kingdoms under my dominion."

She remains in Jerusalem for six months and then sends a message to Solomon, saying, "For the sake of my people, I wish to return to my own country."

Solomon ponders in his heart and says, "A woman of great beauty has come to me. Perhaps God will give me seed in her." For Solomon had married women from all the nations, saying, "My children shall inherit the cities of those nations and shall destroy those who worship idols."

Solomon gives a royal farewell banquet for the Queen of Sheba. When all the servants have departed and they were alone, he goes to her and says, "Sleep here until morning for love's sake."

She answers him, "Swear to me that you will not take me by force and I will swear to you that I will not take any of your possessions by force." He swears to her and she swears to him.

The Queen falls asleep, but she soon awakens with a mouth dry from thirst, for Solomon had given her salty food at the banquet. Before she slept, Solomon had placed a bowl of water and a cup by her bed. She takes a cupful of water and is about to drink when Solomon appears and says, "Why have you broken your oath not to take by force anything that is in my house?"

The Queen says, "I have sinned against myself, but let me drink some water to satisfy my thirst." Solomon answers her, "Am I then also free from the oath which you made me swear?" And the Queen says, "You are free from your oath, but let me drink." He lets her drink some water and afterwards they sleep together and conceive a child.

Before she leaves, Solomon gives her the ring from his little finger, and says, "Take this so you do not forget me. And if it happens that I obtain seed from you, this ring shall be a sign. And if it be a boy, he shall come to me. May God be with you. Go in peace."

The Queen of Sheba leaves Jerusalem and travels home. Nine months and five days later she gives birth to Menelik, a son who resembles Solomon. Upon his twenty-third birthday, he tells his mother that he desires to go to his father, King Solomon. His mother, the queen, gives him the ring Solomon gave her as a sign.

The narrative continues by stating that in those days, King Solomon had no children, except a seven year old boy whose name was Rehoboam.[8] When Menelik appeared before Solomon and showed him the ring, Solomon rejoiced and was thankful to God Who had now given him a son who would rule over the Ark of the Covenant.

The time came for Menelik to return home. He asks Solomon for a small piece of the golden rim of the Ark cover, promising that he and his mother and all his subjects would worship it.[9]

Solomon asks him to remain in Jerusalem, but he says, "It is impossible for me to live here, for you have a son, Rehoboam, who is better than I am, for he was born of your wife lawfully, while my mother is not your wife according to the law."

Before he leaves Jerusalem, Menelik is taken into the Holy of Holies[10] and sovereignty is given to him by the mouth of Zadok, the High Priest and by Joav, the commander of King Solomon's army.[11] They anoint him with the oil of kingship. He emerges from the House of the Lord, and from that time forth, they call his name David.

According to the legend, Solomon sends the firstborn sons of the tribe of Judah to accompany Menelik and dwell with him in the land of Ethiopia. He also sends Azariah, the son of Zadok the High Priest.

---

8. This is incorrect. II Chronicles 12:13 establishes Rehoboam as 25 years old when Sheba visited Solomon. Therefore, Menelik's trip to Jerusalem would have taken place after Solomon had been dead for seven years.

9. This, of course, is idolatry and indicates that the text of the legend as it has come down to us combines monotheism with pagan worship.

10. This is another error. Only the Jewish High Priest is permitted to enter the Holy of Holies and only on Yom Kippur. The kings of the House of David were not anointed in the Temple, but by Gihon Spring, a pool of water outside the walls of Jerusalem. See I Kings 1:33,34.

11. This, too, is an error. Joav was David's military commander, not Solomon's. Joav was executed for treason at the beginning of Solomon's reign by Benaiah ben Jehoiada, Solomon's new military commander. See I Kings 2:28-34.

Azariah says to the others, "An angel appeared to me and instructed me to take the Holy Ark of the Law of God. For the people Israel has provoked God to wrath, and for this reason He will make the Holy Ark of God depart from them."

That night, Azariah and three of his friends make a wooden version of the Ark and go the Holy Temple. Miraculously, they find all the doors open, both those that were outside and those that led into the Holy of Holies. Directed by an angel, they replace the real Ark with the wooden one and leave. The legend states that if it had not been the will of God, the Holy Ark could not have been taken away. And all of this, including the removal of the Ark, was done without Menelik's knowledge.

When he and the sons of Judah depart from Jerusalem, they say to him, "Shall we reveal to you something? Can you keep a secret?"

And he answers them, "Yes, I can keep a secret. If you will tell it to me I will never repeat it till the day of my death."

They tell him they have taken the Holy Ark and it shall be his guide forever, for him and his seed after him if he will only perform the will of the Lord his God. He is warned that he will be unable to take it back even if he wants to, and his father cannot seize it no matter how hard he tries, for the Ark goes of its own free will and it could not have been removed from the Holy of Holies if it did not desire it.

Joyously, Menelik dances around like a lamb, just as his grandfather David danced before the Holy Ark when he took it up to Jerusalem.

They reach the border of Ethiopia without any mishap on the road and all the provinces of Ethiopia rejoice, for the Holy Ark is sending forth a light like that of the sun into the darkness.

That night, Solomon has a dream that the sun came down to Ethiopia and will never return to Judah. Zadok the High Priest understands this to mean the Ark has been taken. He runs to the Holy of Holies and discovers that the Ark is gone.

Solomon pursues Menelik and his party and comes to Gaza. The people inform him that the group of men left nine days earlier and was traveling swifter than eagles. Solomon understands that this was divinely ordained and that he would not be able to recover the Ark.

Solomon laments the loss of the Ark. And it is revealed to him prophetically that it all happened from God. Solomon then says to the priests, "Do not reveal this or else the uncircumcised heathens will glory over us. Let us take the counterfeit wooden Ark and cover it over with gold, and let us lay the Book of the Law inside it. Through this, God will cool His wrath towards us and will not abandon us to our enemies, and He will not remove His mercy from us, but will remember the covenant with our fathers Abraham, Isaac and Jacob."

The legend concludes by saying that the Ark of the Covenant has remained in Ethiopia since that day and there it will stay until Judgment Day when it shall return to Mount Zion even as Moses gave it, and the dead shall be raised and shall live again.

According to its own recorded tradition, Ethiopia has had a dynasty of 225 kings and queens who descended from Solomon and Sheba. This is the longest continuing royal lineage in the history of the world, surviving for nearly 3000 years. The last reigning monarch was Haile Selassie, the Emperor of Ethiopia from 1930 to 1974.

Haile Selassie called himself the "Lion of Judah" in reference to his royal ancestry that traced its line back to King David. The Messianic implications here are obvious.

In 1974, a group of Soviet-backed military officers known as the Derg deposed Haile Selassie and proclaimed the end of the Solomonic dynasty. In August 1975, the Derg announced that Haile Selassie had died in prison of respiratory failure. It is widely assumed that he was assassinated.

The official text of the Ethiopian version of the Solomon and Sheba story is called *Kebra Nagast* (Glory of the Kings). It was adapted from ancient Ethiopian traditions by Christian monks in the 14th century. The *Kebra Nagast* includes a discussion of how the ancient Ethiopians evolved from pagan worship of the sun and the moon and the stars to become servants of the God of Israel and observant of the Torah's commandments for a period of approximately 1200 years.

Around the year 325, King Ezana of Ethiopia converted to Christianity and took his countrymen along with him. From a Jewish perspective, this was a disastrous return to the nation's idolatrous roots. It was as if the merit of the Queen of Sheba had run its course and could no longer sustain the souls of her countrymen with purity.

All references to Ethiopians in this discussion refer to the indigenous Gentile population of Ethiopia. This excludes the community of Ethiopian Jews known as the Beta Israel. These black Jews lived independently of the general Ethiopian society despite a certain amount of assimilation and intermarriage over the centuries. According to Ethiopian Jewish tradition, the Beta Israel were members of the tribe of Dan who migrated to

Ethiopia from the northern kingdom of Israel during an early phase of the First Temple period. Most of the Beta Israel, approximately 130,000 men, women and children, were brought to Israel during the last thirty years of the 20th century, and have assimilated into Israeli society.

It is worth noting that till this day the Ethiopian Orthodox Church is the only Christian sect to include circumcision and Jewish dietary laws as part of its sacramental rites, a holdover from the many centuries that Ethiopians observed the Torah as *Noahide Gerim*.

Jeremiah 3:14

Return backsliding children, says the Lord, for I was a husband to you, and I will take you one from a city and two from a family and I will bring you to Zion.

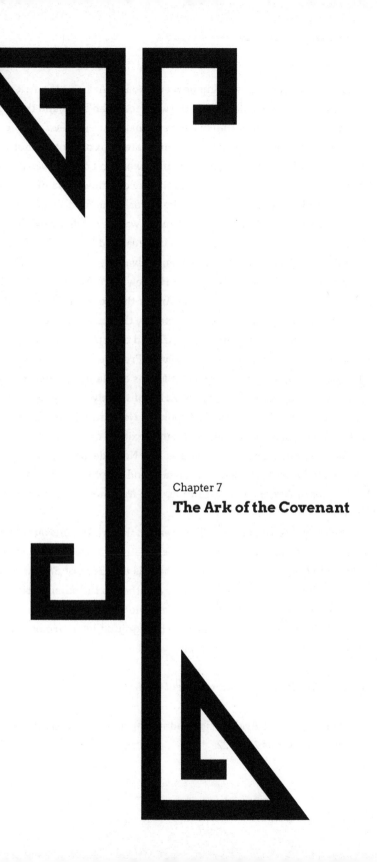

Chapter 7
The Ark of the Covenant

There is a deep relationship between Noah's Ark and the Ark of the Covenant. In the English language, the word for Noah's Ark and the Ark of the Covenant are the same. But in Hebrew, Noah's Ark is a *teva* and the Ark of the Covenant is an *aron*. Both words indicate a box or container of some sort. Noah's Ark was an enormous floating wooden box that was overlaid with tar inside and out for waterproofing. It contained pairs of creatures that God had chosen for salvation in a world doomed to destruction. Paralleling this, the Ark of the Covenant was a wooden box that was overlaid with purest gold inside and out. It testified that God had chosen the Children of Israel for redemption and salvation.

In addition to meaning a box, the Hebrew word for Noah's Ark, *teva*, means a written word. Similarly, the Ark of the Covenant contained the words of the Ten Commandments, written by the finger of God.

The differences between Noah's Ark and the Ark of the Covenant are as striking as their similarities. The Divine Presence was revealed by the Ark of the Covenant, for God spoke to Moses and later prophets of Israel from between the cherubim atop the Ark. Conversely, the Divine Presence was concealed by Noah's Ark. God spoke to Noah only before he entered the Ark and not again until He told Noah to exit the Ark.

The Ark of the Covenant is vital to the Noahide, perhaps even more than Noah's Ark. It is the seat of prophecy, and prophecy is the essence of Noahide Torah. And the Ark testifies that the *Noahide Ger* may rest on the Sabbath.

The Holy Ark was a miraculous creation that transcends our physical world and yet resides within it.[1] By contemplating its structure and nature, we bring the light of the Holy Ark, which is the Light of *Shechina*, into the world, first in our minds and hearts and then to the outside. Time and space are irrelevant here. This is the dimension of soul.

With this relevance to the Ger as a background, let us explore the Ark of the Covenant from several perspectives.

Part one: The Design and Structure of the Ark

The details of the Ark's design and structure were decreed by God and are written in Exodus 25:10-22.

---

1. This will be explained later.

The Ark was a wooden box sandwiched between two boxes of pure gold. The middle wooden box was made of acacia wood and was open at the top. Its length was 2½ cubits by 1½ cubits by 1½ cubits. This is approximately 150 cm (59.1 in.) by 90 cm (35.4 in.) by a height of 90 cm (35.4 in.).[2] A box of pure gold was fitted inside the wooden box, and these two boxes were then placed inside an outer box of pure gold. The walls of the outer gold box were one handbreadth (10 cm or 3.9 in.) higher than walls of the wooden box.

Atop the rim of the outer gold box was a decorative gold crown (*zer*). The rim atop the wooden box was also covered with gold so that no wood showed anywhere on the Ark.

Four gold rings were attached to the width of the Ark, two rings on one side and two rings on the other side. A pole of acacia wood plated with gold was inserted through each pair of rings. The Ark was carried by these two poles.

A solid gold cover called the *Capporet* (Atonement) was made to sit atop the Ark, fitting its length and width precisely. The Ark-cover was one handbreadth thick. The crown atop the rim of the outer gold box rose slightly above the base of the Ark-cover.

Two golden cherubim stood at the ends of the Ark-cover, one cherub at either end, facing each other and looking down towards the Ark-cover. The two cherubim were made in the form of the angels that guard the way to the Tree of Life in the Garden of Eden.[3] The head of each cherub had human facial features and bird-like wings. Their feet were also bird-like.

---

2. Babylonian Talmud, Yoma 72b, the opinion of Rebbe Meir. Our figures are calculated based on a cubit measuring 60 centimeters or 23.6 inches.

3. Genesis 3:24.

From head to shoulders they looked like humans, but from their wings downward, they had the appearance of birds.[4]

The two cherubim were not made separately and then connected to the cover, but were hammered out of the same immense ingot of gold as the Ark-cover itself, so that it was all one piece. The wings of the cherubim spread upwards and outwards, sheltering the entire Ark-cover from above. It was from between the wings of the cherubim that the Voice of God spoke to Moses and the later prophets of Israel.

Inside the Ark rested the two tablets of the Ten Commandments, written in stone by the finger of God, as it says (Exodus 25:16), *"And you will place the Testimony which I shall give you into the Ark."*

Thus, the construction of the Ark of the Covenant was completed, all according to the Word of God.

The Nature of the Ark

The Ark was above nature clothed in nature. It was a physical object crafted by Betzalel the son of Uri of the tribe of Judah, according to instructions given by God to Moses atop Mount Sinai.

Betzalel built and supervised the other builders of the Tabernacle, as it says:

Exodus 31:2

See, I have called by name Betzalel the son of Uri the son of Hur of the tribe of Judah. And I have filled him with the spirit of God, with wisdom and understanding and knowledge, and with every type of workmanship to comprehend skillful works, to work in gold and in silver and in brass and in cutting stones for setting and in carving wood, to accomplish every type of workmanship.

The Talmud[5] tells us that Betzalel was 13 years old when he built the Ark.

---

4. Rabbi Avraham ben Rambam.

5. Babylonian Talmud, Sanhedrin 69b.

Betzalel did not merely build with the skill of a master craftsman. He was endowed with Divine wisdom and knew how to contemplate and permute the letters of Creation, so as to prepare a dwelling place for God, the Eternal, on earth. Building a House for the Infinite to reside in a finite world was itself a miracle. The Ark of the Covenant was the essence of this miracle.

The Tabernacle was a portable Temple of God that moved with the Children of Israel throughout the forty years of their wandering through the desert. The Ark led the way, carried by four Levites. If we calculate the weight of the Ark, we will quickly realize that four men could not possibly have lifted it, let alone carry it through the burning heat of the Sinai desert. The density of pure gold is 19.3 grams per cubic centimeter. With a measurement of 150 cm by 90 cm by 10 cm, the Ark-cover alone was 135,000 cubic centimeters, a weight of 2,605.50 kilos or 5,732.1 lbs. And this is without the cherubim or the Ark and Tablets, which would have brought the total weight of the Ark to almost three metric tons. Not only would it have been impossible for four men to carry it, but if they attempted to lift it, the enormous weight of the Ark would have snapped its slender poles like two matchsticks.

What really happened is that the Ark carried the Levites, whisking them along the desert floor without their feet touching the ground,[6] as it says:

Joshua 4:11
And it was, when all the people had completely passed over [the Jordan], that the Ark of the Lord passed over, and the priests, in the presence of the people.

The Ark passed over of its own accord and took the priests along for the ride.

The Ark traveled ahead of the Children of Israel, clearing the way for the nation as lightning-like bolts of energy shot forth from it, eliminating

6. Babylonian Talmud, Sota 35a.

snakes and scorpions, raising valleys and lowering mountains as it moved along.[7]

When King Solomon moved the Ark into the Holy of Holies of the First Temple, they came to realize that the Ark occupied no space on earth. The Holy of Holies was a chamber 20 cubits wide. They measured from one wall to the Ark and the measurement was 10 cubits. Then they measured from the other side of the Ark to the opposite wall, and it also measured 10 cubits. But the Ark itself was 2½ cubits wide!

This meant that the physical world had no grasp on the Ark. Between the wings atop the Ark, God's Presence on earth was the same as in heaven. In the language of Kabbalah, this is Crown (*Keter*), a spiritual level where Creator and creation, Infinite and finite, exist as one.

This largely explains this reason for the two cherubim atop the Ark. They were a focal point of meditation that led to prophecy. By focusing his thoughts between the wings of the cherubim on the Ark, the prophet was able to ascend to the path of the Tree of Life, as it says (Genesis 3:24), *"And He placed at the east of the Garden of Eden the cherubim and the flaming sword which turned every way to guard the way to the Tree of Life."* The flaming sword is the person's intellect which can either block the way or, when his thoughts are purified, allow the prophet to gain access to the Tree of Life and the state of prophecy.[8]

And when God sent a prophetic message to Moses and the later prophets, it followed the same path, first passing through the angelic cherubim on high and then through the cherubim on the Ark. Thus, the space between the wings of the cherubim was the source of all prophetic inspiration.

This meditative "looking" at the Ark was only in the prophet's mind's-eye, for actually viewing the Ark was fraught with danger, as we shall learn later.

All of this is particularly relevant to the *Noahide Ger*, whose spiritual path is largely contemplative, for it is well-known that the students of the

---

7. Midrash Tanhuma, Vayakhel 7.

8. Sefer Hatzeruf 2b.

Yeshiva of Shem and Eber were great prophets and meditators.[9] And as we approach the Final Redemption, we yearn to fulfill the words of the prophet (Joel 3:1). *"And it will come to pass that I will pour My spirit upon all flesh, and your sons and daughters will prophesy; your elders will dream prophetic dreams and your young men will see visions."*

Chronicles of the Holy Ark: Part One – Mount Sinai

On the 51st day after the Exodus from Egypt, early in the morning on the 6th day of Israel's encampment at Mount Sinai, God said all the words of the Ten Commandments in the presence of all the Children of Israel.[10]

The First Forty Days on the Mountain

On the very next day, the Lord said to Moses:

"Come up to Me on the mountain and remain there and I will give you the tablets of stone and the law and the commandment which I have written so that you may teach them."[11]

And Moses went up onto the mountain and the cloud of glory covered the mountain six days; and on the seventh day, God called to Moses from the midst of the cloud. And the appearance of the glory of the Lord was like a devouring fire atop the mountain in the eyes of the Children of Israel. And Moses entered the cloud and was on the mountain forty days and forty nights.[12] And he did not eat bread or drink water.[13]

---

9. Genesis 10:25, Rashi; Genesis 25:22, Rashi, Rashbam; Yalkut Shimoni, Numbers 22. And many more places.

10. Exodus 20:1; Deuteronomy 9:10.

11. Exodus 24:12,13.

12. Exodus 24:15-18.

13. Deuteronomy 9:9.

And when He finished speaking to him on Mount Sinai, He gave to Moses the two Tablets of Testimony, tablets of stone, written by the finger of God.[14]

And Hashem said to Moses, "Go down, for your people that you brought up from the land of Egypt have become corrupt. They have turned away quickly from the path that I commanded them. They have made a molten calf and bowed down to it and sacrificed to it, and they said, 'This is your god, O Israel, which brought you up out of the land of Egypt.'"[15]

And Moses turned and went down from the mountain with the two tablets of testimony in his hand, tablets that were written on both sides, from one side through to the other side they were written. And the tablets were the work of God and the writing was the writing of God, engraved upon the tablets.[16]

And it came to pass as he drew close to the camp that he saw the calf and the dancing and Moses's anger flared up and he threw the tablets from his hands and broke them at the foot of the mountain.

And he took the calf which they had made and burnt it with fire and ground it to powder and scattered it on the water and made the Children of Israel drink it.[17]

Then Moses stood at the gate of the camp and said, "Whoever is for *Hashem* come to me." And all the sons of Levi gathered to him,[18] and he said to them, "Thus says *Hashem*, the God of Israel, each man place his sword on his thigh and go around from gate to gate in the camp and each man slay his brother and his friend and his relative [who had worshipped the

---

14. Exodus 31:18.

15. Exodus 32:7,8.

16. Exodus 32:15,16.

17. Exodus 32:19,20.

18. None of the Levites nor any of the Israelite women had worshipped the calf.

calf]." And the sons of Levi did according to the word of Moses and there fell of the people that day around 3000 men.[19]

The Second Forty Days on the Mountain

The next day Moses returned to *Hashem* atop the mountain to seek forgiveness for the people's sin. And he fell down in prayer before *Hashem* and he pleaded with Him not to destroy the people, His inheritance, but forgive them and continue to accompany them with His Presence.

After forty days of prayer, Moses received God's forgiveness and promise to keep His Presence with the people to distinguish them from all the other nations on earth. And Moses went down from the mountain.

The Third Forty Days on the Mountain

At that time, God said to Moses:[20]

"Carve for yourself two tablets of stone like the first ones and come up to me onto the mountain. And make for yourself an ark of wood.[21] And I will write on the tablets the words that were on the first tablets which you broke and you shall put them in the ark. So I made an ark of acacia wood and carved two tablets of stone like the first ones and went up onto the mountain with the two tablets in my hands. And He wrote on the tablets according to the first writing, the Ten Commandments which the Lord had spoken to all of you on the mountain out of the midst of the fire in the day of the assembly and the Lord gave them to me. And I turned and came down from the mountain and put the tablets in the ark which I had made and they were there as the Lord commanded."

19. Exodus 32:26-28.

20. Deuteronomy 10:1-5.

21. This is a temporary ark made by Moses to contain the Tablets until the permanent Ark was made by Betzalel.

When Moses came down from the mountain with the Second Tablets, he called to Aaron and the leaders of the congregation and all the Children of Israel came to him and Moses spoke to them and told them that God had forgiven them.[22]

That day became commemorated as Yom Kippur, the Day of Atonement.

Building the Tabernacle

The next day, God said to Moses:

> "Speak to the people to bring freewill offerings of gold and silver and brass and blue and purple and scarlet wool and fine linen and goats' hair and red-dyed rams' skins and *tachash* skins and acacia wood and oil and spices, onyx stones and precious stones. And let them build Me a Sanctuary and I will dwell among them."[23]

God had commanded them to build the Tabernacle, a portable Temple which was to be the dwelling place of the Divine Glory, which is the Ark of the Covenant, as He said to Moses, *"And there I will meet with you and I will speak with you from atop the Ark-cover."* Therefore, He commanded them to build the Ark first, for it is first in importance and the reason for the Tabernacle.[24]

The Tabernacle is completed

> On the first day of the first month of the second year after leaving Egypt, Moses took the tablets out of the wooden ark that he had made and that had been kept in his tent since he came down from the mountain on Yom Kippur. And he put the tablets in the golden Ark that Betzalel made. And he put the poles in

---

22. Exodus 34:31,32. Ibid, *Rashi.*

23. Exodus 25:1-8.

24. Exodus 25:10, commentary of the *Ramban.*

the rings on the Ark and placed the Ark-cover upon the Ark and brought the Ark into the Holy of Holies of the Tabernacle and placed the partition curtain in front of the Ark.[25]

And the cloud covered the Tent of Meeting and the glory of the Lord filled the Tabernacle. And Moses was not able to enter into the Tent of Meeting because the cloud rested upon it and the glory of the Lord filled it.[26] And the cloud of the Lord was upon the Tabernacle by day and there was fire upon it at night in the sight of all the House of Israel throughout their journeys.[27]

The total period of time from the Revelation on Mount Sinai to the completion of the Tabernacle whose primary purpose was to house the Ark of the Covenant was 295 days, the numerical value of the Hebrew word, *ratzah*, to be forgiven.

Chronicles of the Holy Ark: Part Two – Entering the Land

It was one month after the death of Moses, forty years after the Exodus from Egypt. Joshua was the new leader of Israel. He and the entire nation were encamped near the east bank of the Jordan River, waiting to enter the land. The Ark of the Covenant was there with them in fulfillment of God's promise to Moses that His Divine Presence would continue to dwell among the people.

God tells Joshua, *"Arise and cross this Jordan, you and the entire nation, to the land which I am giving to the Children of Israel. This scroll of the Torah shall not leave your mouth, meditate in it day and night so that you observe to do all that is written in it, for then you will succeed in all your ways and then you will prosper."*[28]

Joshua sent two men to spy out the land and Jericho, the walled fortress city, which stood opposite them across the Jordan.

---

25. Exodus 40:20,21.

26. Exodus 40:34,35.

27. Exodus 40:34,35.

28. Joshua 1:2,8.

The spies came to the house of Rahab, a notorious courtesan. She was the perfect source to offer intel to the spies. Her clientele were princes and dignitaries who revealed everything to her. According to the Talmud,[29] Rahab was one of the four most beautiful women who ever lived. And now, God has called her and she answers His call by rejecting Canaanite idolatry and leaving her sordid way of life to become the first *Ger Tzedek* to greet the Children of Israel as they enter the land.

The king of Jericho has learned that the spies have come to Rahab's house and demands that she bring them forth. But at risk to her life, she hides them, telling the king's men that the spies just left and if they pursue them quickly they will catch them, and they run off. Now, God places His spirit upon her and she says to the spies, *"I know that the Lord has given you the land and that the hearts of all the inhabitants of the land have melted because of you, for the Lord your God is God in heaven above and on the earth beneath."*[30]

Her words are an expression of Elijah's promise, *"I call on heaven and earth to bear witness that any individual, man or woman, Jew or Gentile, freeman or slave, can have Ruach Hakodesh (the Holy Spirit) bestowed upon him. It all depends on his deeds."*[31]

The spies elude their pursuers and promise Rahab that she and her family will be saved when the Israelites enter the land to conquer it.

The spies return to Joshua and tell him, "God has delivered all the land into our hands and all its inhabitants have melted away because of us."

The next day, Joshua moved the entire nation, no fewer than two million people, to the east bank of the Jordan and told them, "Prepare yourselves, for tomorrow the Lord will do wonders for you."

The next morning, the priests carried the Ark before the people to the very edge of the river. It was just five days before Passover. During much of the year, the Jordan is a humble little stream, barely a trickle in some places. But the winter rains and melted snow from Mount Hermon have

---

29. Megillah 15a.

30. Joshua 2:9,11.

31. Introduction to *Etz Chaim*, p. 18.

swelled the Jordan and caused it to overflow its banks, turning it into a fast-moving river.

The Talmud[32] states that after the people had all crossed over, the priests carrying the Ark stepped backwards onto the bank from which they had entered, and the waters returned to their natural flow leaving the Ark on one side of the river in full view of all the people on the other side. And then the Ark picked up its bearers and carried them over the Jordan. It was a miracle that proclaimed the glory of the Lord in the same manner as the splitting of the Red Sea. And God showed the people that He was with Joshua just as He had been with Moses.

The Red Sea was deep and calm and the Jordan was shallow and swift, but to God for whom darkness is the same as light,[33] they both revealed the glory of God.

At God's command, Joshua circumcised the men who had been born in the wilderness. During their wanderings, the Israelites were afraid to circumcise their babies because of the danger from desert winds and uncertainty of when they were going to travel. But encamped with the Ark in Gilgal just over the Jordan,[34] they celebrated Passover with the Paschal lamb and ate matzah made from the grain of the land. And they were secure.

But Israel's glorious entrance to the land was not yet complete. There was one stupendous event to take place – the conquest of Jericho, an impregnable fortress city with walls as thick as they were high and massive iron-clad gates.[35] No other Canaanite city was as fortified as Jericho. If the Israelites could conquer and destroy Jericho and its idol-

---

32. Sota 35a.

33. Psalm 139:12.

34. There are two cities called Gilgal, one near the west bank of the Jordan River, the other some 72 kilometers to the west. It is an incorrect view that the Israelites miraculously traveled to the distant Gilgal that first day, for the verse (Joshua 4:19) states that *"they camped in Gilgal at the eastern border of Jericho,"* which is barely three kilometers west of the Jordan.

35. Talmud, Berachot 54b.

worshipping populace, God's promise to give the land of the Canaanites, Hittites, Amorites, Perizzites, Jebusites, Hivvites, and Girgashites to the children of Abraham, Isaac and Jacob would begin with majesty and a show of invincible power.

God commanded Joshua to assemble 20,000 Israelite soldiers, followed by seven priests with rams' horns, followed by the Ark of the Covenant, followed by a rear guard of another 20,000 Israelite warriors. They were to walk around the walls of Jericho silently except for the priests blowing their ram's horns. For each of six days, the procession quietly marched once around the walls of Jericho with ram's horns blaring. On the seventh day, they encircled the walls seven times. The only sound heard was the blast of the ram's horns. Then, after the seventh circling, Joshua called to the people, *"Shout, for the Lord has given you the city."* And all the people shouted with a great shout and the indestructible walls of Jericho collapsed. They did not topple over, but sank down into the earth where they stood. And the Israelite warriors charged in and took the city.

Joshua spoke to the two men who had spied out the region, and told them, *"Go to Rahab's house and rescue her and all the members of her family and place them just outside the camp of Israel."*

After Jericho was destroyed, Joshua brought Rahab into his tent as his wife. Eight prophets and priests were among her descendants.[36] And she dwelled in the midst of Israel for the rest of her life.

The Tabernacle was erected in Gilgal where it remained for fourteen years during which time the Israelites conquered and divided the land. And then they moved the Tabernacle and the Ark to Shiloh. They stood in Shiloh for 369 years.[37]

Chronicles of the Holy Ark: Part Three – Eli and his Sons

Eli was the High Priest and a prophet who judged Israel during the last forty years that the Tabernacle stood at Shiloh.

---

36. Megillah 14b. Rebbe Judah says that there was a ninth descended from her, the Prophetess Hulda.

37. *Mishneh Torah*, Laws of the Temple 1:2.

Tragically, Eli's two sons, Hofni and Phineas, had disgraced the priesthood by failing to show proper respect for God and profaning the sanctity of the sacrificial offerings.[38]

> And the Lord called to Samuel the Prophet from out of the Holy of Holies of the Tabernacle where stood the Ark.[39]
>
> And Lord said to Samuel, "Behold, I am about to do something in Israel which will make the ears tingle of everyone who hears it."[40]
>
> And the Philistines amassed against Israel and the battle ensued and Israel was beaten before the Philistines, and they slew on the field of battle about four thousand men.
>
> And the elders of Israel said, "Why has the Lord beaten us today before the Philistines? Let us take the Ark of the Covenant of the Lord from Shiloh and He will come in our midst and save us from the hand of our enemies." And the people sent to Shiloh and from there they carried the Ark of the Covenant of the Lord of Hosts Who dwells between the cherubim. And with the Ark of the Covenant of God were Eli's two sons, Hofni and Phineas.
>
> And it was when the Ark of the Lord's Covenant came into the camp that all Israel shouted a great shout and the earth stirred. And the Philistines heard the sound of the shouting and they said, "What is the sound of the great shout in the camp of the Hebrews?" And they knew that the Ark of the Lord had come into the camp. And they said, "Woe is us, for there never was anything like this yesterday or any other day. Woe is to us. Who will save us from the hand of this mighty God? This is the God who smote the Egyptians with every kind of plague in the wilderness. Strengthen yourselves and become men, you Philistines, lest you serve the Hebrews as they have served you, you must become men and fight."

---

38. 1 Samuel 2:12, commentaries of *Radak, Ralbag.*

39. Ibid. 3:4.

40. Ibid. 3:11.

And the Philistines waged war and Israel was beaten and they fled each man to his tents. Now the blow was very great and there fell from Israel thirty thousand infantrymen. And the Ark of God was captured and the two sons of Eli, Hofni and Phineas, were slain.

And a man [of the tribe] of Benjamin ran from the battlefield and came to Shiloh on that day with his garments torn and earth upon his head. And he came and, behold, Eli was sitting on the chair anxiously waiting, for his heart trembled concerning the Ark of God. And the man had come to tell [the news] in the city and the whole city cried out.

Eli heard the sound of the cry and said, "What is this confused noise?" And the man hurried and came to tell Eli.

Now Eli was ninety-eight years old and his eyes were set and he could not see. And the man said to Eli, "I am the one who has come from the battlefield and I fled from the battle today."

And he said, "What happened, my son?" And the one who had reported the news answered and said, "Israel fled before the Philistines and also there was a great slaughter among the people and your two sons are dead and the Ark of God was captured."

And it was when he mentioned the Ark of God that he [Eli] fell off the chair backwards through the gate opening and broke his neck and he died.

And when his daughter-in-law, the wife of Hofni, heard the news of the Ark, she went into labor and died in childbirth, but before she died, she said, "Glory has been exiled from Israel, for the Ark of God has been taken."[41]

Now, the Philistines took the Ark of God and brought it to the house of *Dagon* (their idol) and set it up beside Dagon. And the Ashdodites arose early the next day and behold *Dagon* had fallen face downward to the ground before the Ark of the Lord and they returned the idol to its place.

And they arose early the next morning and, behold, *Dagon* had fallen face downward to the ground before the Ark of the Lord and *Dagon's* head and the two palms of his hands were cut

---

41. 1 Samuel 4:3-22.

off and were lying on the threshold and only the body of *Dagon* remained on him.[42]

And the hand of the Lord became heavy on the Ashdodites and struck them with hemorrhoids, Ashdod and those on its borders.

And the people said, "Let not the Ark of the God of Israel dwell with us, for His hand is harsh upon us and upon *Dagon*, our god."[43]

And they brought the Ark of the God of Israel to Gath. And the hand of the Lord was upon the city with a great panic and He struck the people of the city, young and old, with hemorrhoids in the hidden parts of their bodies.

And they sent the Ark of God to Ekron and the Ekronites cried out, "They have brought around the Ark of the God of Israel to kill our people."[44]

And the Ark of the Lord was in the field of the Philistines for seven months and mice infested the field and ate the crops.[45]

So the lords of the Philistines made a cart out of wood and hitched two milk cows to it and kept their calves away from them.

And they placed the Ark of the Lord on the cart and next to it they placed a box with offerings of five gold figures of hemorrhoids and five gold figures of mice and sent the cart away. And the cows went straight up the road to Beth Shemesh and the chiefs of the Philistines knew it was from the Lord because milking cows would not normally leave their calves.[46]

Now, the people of Beth Shemesh were reaping the wheat harvest in the valley and they lifted up their eyes and saw the [uncovered] Ark and they rejoiced to see it [for this meant that

---

42. 1 Samuel 5:3,4.

43. Ibid. 5:6,7.

44. Ibid. 5:10.

45. 1 Samuel 6:1, commentary of *Ralbag*.

46. Ibid. 6:7-12.

it had returned to Israel]. And the cart had come to the field of Joshua of Beth Shemesh.[47]

And the Levites took down the Ark of the Lord and the box containing the golden objects and they placed the Ark on a great boulder that stood in the field of this Joshua.

And they split the wood of the cart and offered up the cows as a burnt offering to the Lord.

And He smote the men of Beth Shemesh for they had gazed upon the Ark of the Lord, and He smote seventy men and fifty thousand men and the people mourned, for the Lord had struck them with a great blow.[48]

The Rabbis of the Talmud[49] offer several views as to what the people of Beth Shemesh had done to deserve such a catastrophic punishment.

One opinion is that they continued the work of reaping and binding the wheat instead of stopping and honoring the Ark. Another one says that they spoke disdainfully, implying that God lacked the power to prevent the Ark from being captured by the Philistines. And a third opinion was that the people looked inside the Ark, which was the ultimate of disrespect.

But if we hold to the simple meaning of the verse, we must conclude that God struck the people for no other reason than *"they had gazed upon the Ark of the Lord."* Targum Yonatan translates it, *"and they rejoiced and gazed."*

At first glance, this seems like an overly harsh punishment. But the Torah gave us fair warning when the Ark traveled during the years in the wilderness, as it says (Numbers 4:5,6), *"When the camp is preparing to move, Aaron and his sons shall come and remove the curtain[50] and drape it over the Ark of Testimony with it. And they shall put on top of it a covering of tachash skin and spread a blue cloth over it."* A few verses

---

47. Ibid. 13,14.

48. Ibid. 6:19.

49. Sotah 35a?

50. This is the *Parochet*, the curtain that separates the Holy of Holies (where the Ark is) from the other part of the Tent of Meeting.

later, it says (Numbers 4:20), *"But they shall not come in to see when the holy objects are covered or else they will die."*

We learn from this that whenever the Ark traveled, it was completely covered and no one saw it. Even the priests who covered the Ark were warned not to look at it or they would die.

But the men of Beth Shemesh gazed at the Ark and upon the *Shechina* Who dwells between the cherubim atop the Ark and they paid for it with their lives.

How can we understand this? Imagine the Sun compacting itself with all its energy into an area the size of a refrigerator standing in front of you a few meters away. The temperature at the surface of the Sun is ten million degrees and twenty-seven million degrees at its core. How long would you last in the presence of that fire and blinding light?

Now, imagine the Source of the Sun and of all the stars of all the galaxies, "Who spoke and brought the universe into being," constricting His Presence between the cherubim of the Ark. This is what the men of Beth Shemesh gazed upon.

They could have taken a lesson from Noah and his sons. When Noah became inebriated from wine and lay naked in his tent, his son Ham came in and stared at him, and his offspring were cursed for it. Noah's other two sons, Shem and Japheth, entered carrying a garment and covered their father with it; *"their faces were turned away from Noah and they saw not their father's nakedness."*[51] And for their modest behavior, they received Noah's blessing.

The men of Beth Shemesh stared at their heavenly Father's nakedness in this world and paid for it with their lives.

The Midrash tells us that the people of Beth Shemesh should have closed their eyes as soon as they saw the Ark, and then prostrated themselves before it with their faces pressed to the ground until someone brought a garment to cover it. And then, the Name of God would be have been sanctified throughout the world.[52] Whoever has learned the First Book of Samuel would know this.

51. Genesis 9:23.

52. Exodus Rabba.

Chronicles of the Holy Ark: Part Four – David

And the men of Beth Shemesh asked, "Who can go stand before the Lord, this holy God? And where will the Ark go when it leaves us?"

And they sent messengers to the residents of Kiriath-Jearim, saying, "The Philistines have returned the Ark of the Lord. Come down, and take it up to you."[53]

And the men of Kiriath-Jearim came and took up the Ark of the Lord and brought it to the house of Abinadab on the hill, and they appointed Elazar, his son, to watch over the Ark of the Lord. And from the day that the Ark was housed in Kiriath-Jearim, there passed many days, a period of twenty years, during which the entire house of Israel was loyal to the Lord.[54]

By this time, David was king over Israel, a king whose chief priority was to find the site where the Holy Temple would be built.[55]

David wrote (Psalms 132:4)

I will not give sleep to my eyes nor rest to my eyelids, until I find the place for God, a dwelling for the Mighty One of Jacob.

And David made for himself houses in the city of David and he prepared a place for the Ark of God and he pitched a tent for it.[56]

---

53. The people of Kiriath-Jearim were more God fearing and more learned in Torah than the men of Beth Shemesh and would care for the Ark appropriately and, therefore, safely.

54. 1 Samuel 6:20,21; Ibid., 7:1,2. Kiriath-Jearim is a Judean town approximately 26 km (15 mi.) from Beth Shemesh and 16 km (9.5 mi) from Jerusalem.

55. That is, a permanent home for the Ark of the Covenant, in contrast to the Tabernacle which had always been a temporary residence.

56. 1 Chronicles 15:1

And David arose and went with all the people who were with him, from Baale-Judah[57] to bring up from there the Ark of God, the name of which is the Name of the Lord of Hosts Who dwells upon its cherubim.

Had David remained in Hebron, where he first established his kingship, he would never have aspired to take the Ark out of Kiriath-Jearim to bring it close to him. But when he moved his throne to Jerusalem, he was the anointed of God in the city of God. In Jerusalem, David became the custodian of the Ark, a distinction he shared with no one before him or after him.

> And they set the Ark of God upon a new cart and they carried it from the house of Abinadab on the hill; and Uzzah and Ahio,[58] the sons of Abinadab, drove the new cart.[59]
>
> And David and the house of Israel were joyful before the Lord, playing upon all kinds of instruments of cypress wood and harps and lutes and drums and tambourines and cymbals.
>
> And they came as far as Goren-Nachon and Uzzah stretched out his hand to the Ark of God and seized hold of it to steady it for the oxen had caused it to shake.
>
> And the anger of the Lord was kindled against Uzzah and God struck him down there for his misdeed and he died there by the Ark of God.
>
> Afterwards David said, "It is not proper to carry the Ark of God except by the Levites, for the Lord chose them to carry the Ark and to serve Him forever."[60]

David had assumed that the Ark was to be carried by Levites only in the generation of the Exodus, for that generation was on a high spiritual

---

57. Another name for Kiriath-Jearim.

58. Brothers of Elazar, who had been guardian of the Ark.

59. It is presumed that the Ark was covered and hidden from view.

60. I Chronicles 15:2.

level. But since the people of David's generation were on a lower level, he felt that no one was fit to carry the Ark, so it needed to be placed on a cart.[61]

> And David held off bringing the Ark of the Lord to him in the city of David. And David took it to the house of Oved-Edom the Gittite.[62]
>
> And the Ark of the Lord dwelled in the house of Oved-Edom the Gittite for three months, and the Lord blessed Oved-Edom and his household.[63]
>
> And then, David removed the Ark of God from the house of Oved-Edom and brought it into the city of David with joy.
>
> And David danced with all his might before the Lord and David was girded with a linen tunic.
>
> And David and all the house of Israel brought up the Ark of the Lord with shouts of joy and the call of the ram's horn.
>
> And it came to pass when God helped the Levites, the bearers of the Ark of the Covenant, that they sacrificed seven bulls and rams.[64]

The phrase, "when God helped the Levites," indicates that the Ark miraculously carried itself and its bearers as in earlier days.[65]

> And they brought the Ark of God and set it up in the midst of the tent that David had pitched for it. And David stationed

---

61. Eliyahu of Vilna.

62. Oved-Edom was a Levite whose sons would be appointed by David as guards at the Temple gates. See I Chronicles 26:4.

63. God blessed Oved-Edom with eight sons who became sentries at the gates of the Temple.

64. I Chronicles 15:26.

65. *Rashi*.

some of the ministering Levites before the Ark to remember and thank and praise the Lord God of Israel.[66]

It is inconceivable that the Levites stood and sang in the presence of the Holy Ark. Rather, the tent must have had partitions and the Levites, though stationed *"before the Ark,"* were on the other side of these partitions.

> And it came to pass when God gave David rest from all his enemies and caused him to dwell securely in his house, David said to Nathan the prophet, "See, I dwell in a house of cedar, but the Ark of God dwells within the curtains [of a tent]."[67]

David felt shame for the opulence in which he lived while the Holy Ark sat in a simple tent.

The Word of God came to Nathan that same night, saying that a House would be built for the Name of God, but David would not build it; a son not yet born to David would build it. This son was Solomon.

Years later, David told Solomon:

> "My son, it was in my heart to build a House in the Name of the Lord, my God. But the Word of the Lord was upon me, saying, 'You have shed much blood and you have waged great wars; you shall not build a House in My Name because you have shed much blood to the ground before Me. Behold, a son will be born to you; he will be a man of peace, and I shall give him peace from all his enemies around, and Solomon will be his name,[68] and I shall give peace and quiet to Israel in his days. He shall build a House in My Name, and he shall be to Me for a son and I will be to him as a Father.'"[69]

---

66. I Chronicles 16:1,4.

67. II Samuel 7:1.

68. Solomon in Hebrew is Shlomo, which translates as "peace is his."

69. I Chronicles 22:6-8.

Even though David was not permitted to build the Temple, he made extensive preparations for it before his death.[70] He dug the Temple's foundations, established the Levites as singers to praise God and made thousands of musical instruments to accompany them. He divided the *Kohanim* into twenty-four watches and set up Levites as sentries at the Temple's gates. He organized the judges and bailiffs into functional divisions. And he wrote down the architectural plans of the Temple that he had received by the hand of God and gave the design to his son Solomon, including the plan of the Holy of Holies where the Ark of the Covenant[71] would rest.

David told Solomon:

"In my poverty, I prepared for the house of the Lord one hundred thousand talents of gold and one million talents of silver, and brass and iron beyond measure for its abundance. I have prepared wood and stone also, and you may add to them. And with you are workmen in abundance, woodworkers and stonecutters, and skillful men for every kind of work. Of gold and silver and bronze and iron there is no limit. Arise and begin work, and may the Lord be with you."[72]

And then, David addressed the entire nation, saying:

"Now place your hearts and your souls to seek the Lord your God. Arise and build the Sanctuary of the Lord God to bring the Ark of the Covenant of the Lord and the holy vessels of God to the House that is to be built in the Name of the Lord."[73]

---

70. I Chronicles 22:2.

71. I Chronicles 22:2.

72. Ibid. 22:14-16.

73. Ibid. 22:19.

But it was David alone who yearned to build the House of God. The rest of the Jewish people showed no interest in the the the Temple.[74] And the anger of God flared up against the nation and He put the idea in David's mind to take a census of the people, a risky act which had been known to cause a plague among the people.[75]

Joav, David's military chief, was fearful of the danger, but reluctantly obeyed the order of the king. He and a corps of census-takers counted the number of men fit for military duty, those between twenty and fifty years old. The tally was one million three hundred thousand men.

> And the Lord sent a pestilence upon Israel from the morning until the appointed time.[76] And there died of the people from Dan to Beersheva seventy thousand men.
>
> And the angel of destruction stretched out his hand towards Jerusalem to destroy it, but God relented and said to the destroying angel, "Enough. Withdraw your hand."
>
> And the angel of the Lord was by the threshing floor of Aravnah the Jebusite.
>
> When David saw the destroying angel among the people, he said to the Lord, "Behold, I have sinned and have acted with iniquity, but this flock what have they done? Please, let Your hand be against me and my father's house."
>
> And the Prophet Gad came to David on that day and said to him, "Go up and erect an altar to the Lord on the threshing floor of Aravnah the Jebusite." And David went up according to the word of Gad as the Lord had commanded.[77]

---

74. The *Ramban's* commentary to Numbers 16.

75. There are several explanations as to why census-taking causes a plague among the Jewish people. Perhaps the most definitive one is that numbering the people is a repudiation of God's promise to Jacob, *"And your seed shall be as the dust of the earth (Genesis 28:14),"* which is beyond counting.

76. According to the Talmud (Berachot 62b) this was a period of six hours.

77. II Samuel 24:15-19.

Aravna[78] the Ger: Gateway to the Holy Temple

And Aravnah saw the king and his servants coming towards him and he bowed down to the king with his face to the ground.

And Aravnah said, "Why has my lord the king come to his servant?"

And David said, "To acquire from you the threshing floor to build an altar to the Lord so the plague that has fallen upon the people will end."

And Aravnah said to David, "Let my lord the king take it and offer up whatever seems good in his eyes. Behold, here are the oxen for the burnt offering and the threshing tools and harness of the oxen for fire wood." All this Aravnah, the king,[79] gave to the king. And Aravnah said to the king, "May the Lord your God accept you."

And the king said to Aravnah, "No, I will only buy it from you for a price; so that I do not offer to the Lord my God burnt offerings for nothing." And David purchased the threshing floor and the oxen for fifty shekels of silver.[80]

And David built there an altar to the Lord and he offered up burnt offerings and peace offerings and he called out to the Lord; and He answered him with fire descending from heaven onto the sacrificial altar. And the Lord commanded the angel to return his sword to its sheath."[81]

And David said, "This is the place of the House of the Lord God and this is the altar for burnt offerings for Israel."[82]

---

78. He is called Aravnah in the Second Book of Samuel, but in the First Book of Chronicles, he is called Ornan, a variant of the name.

79. Aravnah was the Jebusite king.

80. II Samuel 24:20-24.

81. II Chronicles 18:26,27.

82. Ibid. 19:1.

The meeting of David and Aravnah was a defining moment in the advancement of the world. It brought together two kings, one the anointed of God, and the other a Jebusite. What transpired between them stopped a plague that took seventy thousand lives in less than a day. And it was the first step to building God's House on earth.

Actually, it is difficult to understand what Aravnah was doing there in the first place. As a Jebusite, he should have been extinct, as Moses said shortly before the Israelites entered the land, *"When the Lord your God shall bring you into the land where you are going to possess it, and shall cast out many nations before you, the Hittite, and the Girgashite and the Amorite and the Canaanite and the Perizzite and the Hivite and the Jebusite, seven nations greater and mightier than you. And when the Lord your God shall deliver them up before you, then you shall utterly destroy them; you shall make no covenant with them, nor show any mercy to them."*[83]

And yet, more than four hundred years later, we find that Aravnah, the king of the Jebusites, is the sole owner of the choicest piece of real estate in Israel, and God has chosen him to be the gateway to the Holy Temple, just as He had chosen Rahab to be the gateway to the land of Israel.[84]

One might think that David could have fulfilled a positive commandment by simply killing Aravnah the Jebusite on the spot and confiscating his property. But the Talmud tells us that Aravnah was a *Ger Toshav.* Therefore, he was permitted to settle in the land and to receive material and spiritual support from the Jewish people. The *Rambam*[85] explains it according to Jewish Law:

> Do not wage war with any person in the world until you have offered him the opportunity to make peace. And it is the same whether it is a war of conquest or a commanded war.[86] As

---

83. Deuteronomy 7:1.

84. Joshua, 2:1-14.

85. Mishneh Torah, Laws of Kings and their Wars, 6:1.

86. A commanded war refers to the commandment to wipe out the seven Canaanite nations and the Amalekites.

it is written (Deuteronomy 20:10). "When you approach a city to wage war against it, you must call out a proposal of peace." If they agree to the peace offer and accept the Seven Laws that were commanded to the Children of Noah, you must not kill a single soul of them. And they are to pay tribute, as it says,[87] "They shall pay tribute to you and serve you."

In effect, Aravnah had ceased existing as a Jebusite and had become integrated into Israel as a *Ger Toshav*, a Resident Noahide, a companion and brother to the Jewish people.

The first two times that Aravnah's name is mentioned in these verses he is called Aravnah the Jebusite. Seven more times he is mentioned, and in each case he is simply called Aravnah. From the moment Aravnah is associated with the altar of the Lord, he is no longer called a Jebusite. When he bowed down upon the future Holy Temple floor in front of King David, God elevated his soul to a exalted place that it had never known, as it says (Psalms 107:9), *"For He has satisfied the longing soul and has filled the hungry soul with good."*

The Talmud says that Aravnah's skull was found under the Great Altar (*Mizbeyach*) in the Temple courtyard.

The Talmud uses coded language and this statement is not meant to be taken literally. Firstly, Aravnah's skull was firmly attached to his body when he bowed to David and offered his threshing floor as a gift. Secondly, there was no altar on his threshing floor until David built one, so Aravnah's skull could hardly have been found under something that did not exist. What the Talmud means is that Aravnah transcended his nature by freely offering his threshing floor as the place to build an altar to the Lord.

The word for skull used here by the Talmud is *gulgalta*, which in the language of Kabbalah is *Kether*, Crown. It refers to the Godliness that is the soul of man. By helping David acquire the site of the Temple Mount, Aravnah was the essential *Ger Toshav* rising above his nature and affecting the higher worlds.[88] By assisting an Israelite in performance of a *mitzvah*, the Noahide is carried by the *mitzvah* to the Throne of Glory.

---

87. Ibid. 20:11.

88. The other way is by attaining prophecy.

We are told of Aravnah's newly elevated status when God calls him by name and gives him the power to see the angel. His name, Aravnah, is spelled exactly the same as the Hebrew word for the Ark of God, A-R-V-N-H (*Aron Hay*).

Now, why was a threshing floor chosen as the site of the House of God? A threshing floor is the place where wheat is separated from its chaff. This indicates a primary function of the Temple, the removal and elimination of the unclean spiritual husks (*kelipot*) which attach themselves to purity (*tahara*) and holiness (*kedusha*).

David, the Custodian of the Ark

As an aging king, David became deeply absorbed in Torah learning and meditation and turned his focus away from affairs of state. This opened the door for Absalom, one of David's sons, to seek the life of his father in order to seize the throne for himself.

> And David said to all his servants who were with him in Jerusalem, "Arise and let us run, for there will be no escape for us from Absalom. Go quickly before he can hurry and overtake us and bring evil upon us and smite the city with the edge of the sword."[89]

And David and his friends and servants, archers, slingers, and Gittites passed over the Kidron brook on the way to the wilderness.

> And Zadok the Priest was also there and all the Levites with him carrying the Ark of the Covenant; and they set down the Ark of God and Abiathar the High Priest went up to it [and waited] until all the people passed out of the city.
>
> And the king said to Zadok, "Carry the Ark of God back to the city; if I find favor in the eyes of the Lord, then He will bring me back, and He will show it to me and also His Dwelling Place. But if He says, 'I do not want you,' behold, let Him do to me as seems good in his eyes.'"

---

89. II Samuel 15:14

> And the king said to Zadok the priest, "Now, look. Return to
> the city in peace and Ahimaatz your son, and Jonathan the son of
> Abiathar, your two sons, shall be with you. See, I will wait in the
> plains of the wilderness until word of information comes to me
> from you."
>
> And Zadok and Abiathar returned the Ark of God to
> Jerusalem and they remained there. And David ascended to the
> top of the Mount of Olives weeping as he went up and his head
> was covered and he walked barefoot and all the people with him
> went with heads covered and weeping as they ascended.[90]

David placed his trust in God rather than use the Ark for his own
benefit. By so doing, he rectified the catastrophic error that Hofni and
Phineas, the sons of Eli, and the Elders committed two generations earlier
when they took the Ark taken out of the Tabernacle at Shiloh to help them
battle against the Philistines. David's self-sacrifice and supreme trust in
God showed that he alone was worthy of being the custodian of the Holy
Ark.

Part Five: Solomon

When God denied David the privilege of building the Holy Temple, He
revealed the depth of His kindness and love for him. By choosing Solomon
to build the Temple and revealing it to David, God had given him the gift of
nachas.[91]

It is difficult to translate *nachas* from the Hebrew. *Nachas* is the
combination of pride, satisfaction and relief that a parent feels when
his child accomplishes something. It can be a small accomplishment
like learning how to tie his shoes or ride a bicycle. Or it can be a great
accomplishment like saving a life or building the House of God. And it does

---

90. II Samuel 15:24-30.

91. *Nachas* is the Ashkenazic pronunciation. In modern Hebrew it is *nachat*,
but this is one of those words that even the fiercest modern Hebrew linguist
admits can be properly pronounced in this manner. *Nachat* simply does not
give anyone *nachas*.

not have to be a child. It can be a spouse or a student or a loving friend or relative. A person can get *nachas* from almost anyone in the world except himself.

God had informed David of His decision through the Prophet Nathan, who told him, *"When your days are completed and you shall lie with your fathers, then I will raise up your seed that shall proceed from your body after you and I will establish his kingdom. He shall build a House for My Name and I will establish the throne of his kingdom forever."*[92]

> And David went in and sat before the Lord and said, "Who am I, O Lord God, and what is my house that You have brought me this far?[93] And now, O Lord God, the word that You have spoken concerning Your servant and concerning his house, confirm it forever and do as You have spoken."[94]

David lived to see his son sitting on his throne and wearing his crown; and he knew with absolute certainty that Solomon was going to fulfill his greatest dream, to build the House of God. This is *nachas*.

> And God gave Solomon wisdom and exceedingly great understanding and a heart as broad as the sand on the seashore. And Solomon's wisdom was greater than the wisdom of all the children of the east. And he was wiser than all men.[95]

Solomon's lofty ambition was to usher in the Final Redemption by influencing the Gentile nations to reject idolatry and follow the Seven Laws of Noah. He saw himself in the role of the Messiah. And, technically, no one but Solomon would ever be the Messiah, the anointed one, the son of David.

---

92. II Samuel 7:12, 13.

93. II Samuel 7:18.

94. Ibid. 7:25.

95. I Kings 5:9-11.

To accomplish his mission, Solomon devised a fourfold plan. He married princesses from powerful foreign nations, hoping to produce offspring who would grow up to govern their respective people and bring them to righteousness.

And he attracted *Gerim Toshavim* to settle in the land of Israel, all of them loyal servants of God. For the building of the Temple, Solomon employed 150,000 of these *Gerim*, as it says (2 Chronicles 2:16), *"And Solomon counted all the Gerim men who were in the land of Israel after David had counted them and they were found to be 153,600. And he made of them 70,000 who carried loads and 80,000 stonecutters in the mountains and 3,600 overseers to supervise the work."*

And Solomon made a covenant with Hiram, the venerable king of Tyre,[96] to provide lumber for the construction of the Temple. Hiram was a powerful and righteous monarch whose ships ruled the seas. And he was on a towering spiritual level. He was one of the nine people that the Midrash says entered *Gan Eden* without tasting death.[97]

When Solomon wrote to Hiram asking for his friendship and help, Hiram answered, *"Blessed be the Lord this day who has given to David a wise son over this great people."* And Hiram gave Solomon cedar wood and cypress wood according to all his desire.[98]

And, finally, Solomon built the most glorious edifice the world has ever known. He knew that the Holy Temple would attract people from all over the world to come and see the revealed Presence of God. God Himself would do the rest, as it says (Isaiah 2:3), *"And many nations shall go and they shall say, 'Come, let us go up to the mountain of the Lord, to the House of the God of Jacob, and let Him teach us of His ways and we will go in His paths."*

---

96. Lebanon, the country to the north of Israel.

97. Yalkut Shimoni, Ezekiel, chapter 367, section 28.

98. I Kings 5:21, 24.

"And in the 480th year after the Exodus from Egypt, King Solomon begin to build the House of the Lord."[99] He was sixteen years old at the time.[100] It took seven years to complete construction of the Temple. And then, Solomon set in motion the process by which the whole world could be transformed into the Garden of Eden.

"Now all the work that Solomon did for the House of the Lord was completed. And the priests brought the Ark of the Covenant of the Lord to its place to the Debir of the House, to the Holy of Holies."

The Holy of Holies was the resting place of God on earth. It was twenty cubits[101] by twenty cubits by twenty cubits high. In its center was the Foundation Stone. This is Zion, the place that marks the Presence of God. It was upon this stone that the Ark of the Covenant was placed. According to the Talmud,[102] this stone is the center of the world. Creation began with this stone and expanded from there.

And it was under this stone that Jacob slept and dreamed of a ladder reaching from the earth to the heavens with angels of God ascending and descending upon it.

> And behold, the Lord stood above it and said: "I am the Lord, the God of Abraham your father and the God of Isaac. The land upon which you are sleeping I will give to you and to your offspring."[103]
>
> And Jacob awoke from his sleep and he said, "Surely, the Lord is in this place and I knew it not." And he was afraid and

---

99. I Kings 6:1. 480 is the *gematria* (numerical value) of *maasechem*, your deeds, indicating that the Holy Temple was built in the merit of the collective *mitzvoth* that the Israelites did from the time they left Egypt until that day.

100. *Rashi* and many others. According to Josephus he was eighteen years old and Rabbi Isaac Abarbanel maintained that he was twenty-four.

101. A cube approximately 12 meters (40 feet) in length, width and height.

102. Yoma 54b.

103. Genesis 28:13.

said, "How awesome is this place. This is none other than the House of God and this is the gate of heaven."[104]

When the Ark was brought into the Holy of Holies and placed upon the Foundation Stone, heaven and earth were in perfect alignment and the *Shechina* dwelled among Israel as a husband dwells with his wife in their home.

And when the priests who carried the Ark departed from the Holy of Holies, *"the priests could not stand to serve, because the glory of the Lord filled the House of God."*

And Solomon said, *"I have built the House for the Name of the Lord, the God of Israel. And I have set there the Ark wherein is the Covenant of the Lord, which He made with the Children of Israel."*

And Solomon prayed that God answer the prayers of Israel when they are directed towards this House.

And also to the *nochri* (stranger) who is not of Your people Israel, but will come from a distant land because of Your great Name, your strong hand and your outstretched arm, and they will come and pray toward this House. You shall hear from heaven from Your dwelling place and you shall do whatever the stranger calls upon You that all people of the earth may know Your Name to fear You as do Your people Israel.

And when Solomon finished praying, the fire descended from heaven and consumed the burnt offerings and the sacrifices and the glory of the Lord filled the House. And the priests could not enter the House of the Lord because the glory of the Lord filled the House of the Lord. And all the Children of Israel saw the descent of the fire and the glory of the Lord upon the House and they bowed down on their faces to the ground on the floor and they prostrated themselves and said, "Give thanks to the Lord for He is good for His loving kindness is eternal."[105]

---

104. Ibid. 13:16,17.

105. II Chronicles 7:1-4.

Five kings had formed an alliance to build the House of God. They were: God Himself, David, Aravnah, Solomon and Hiram.

Only a king can build or destroy the Holy Temple because the Temple is the essence of Kingdom (*Malchut*) and only Kingdom has the power to reveal the Source of all. The first Temple was built by King Solomon and destroyed by Nebuchadnezzar, king of Babylon. The Second Temple was built by Darius, the king of Persia,[106] and was destroyed by Vespasian, the Emperor of Rome. The Third Temple will be built by the future king of Israel, the Messiah, and it will never be destroyed.[107]

Had the Jewish people remained wholehearted with God, they would have ascended level after level until reaching the final rectification of the sin of Adam in the Garden of Eden. Then the world would have shed its present form and become clothed in a new form, transcending all that had ever existed since the beginning of creation. From this exalted level, there is no descent or failure. But since evil prevailed and the people sinned, the Temple that Solomon built stood for 410 years and was then destroyed.[108]

The people had taken advantage of their great prosperity and had abused God's mercy[109] by betraying Him and turning to idolatry, adultery, and murder, and failing to allow the land rest during the Sabbatical Year.

---

106. Herod, the non-Jewish king of Judea, rebuilt the Second Temple. It is his Temple, an illegal structure, which is described in the Mishna and the *Rambam*.

107. Ezekiel 37:26.

108. *Mishkanay Elyon* of Rabbi Moshe Chaim Luzzatto, (*Ramchal*), *zy"a*.

109. With the Temple standing and the Ark resting in the Holy of Holies, the people's sins were continually forgiven by the daily burnt offering and the Temple incense offering (*ketoret*). When the people slept, they were forgiven for the sins they had committed the previous day and when they were out sinning the next day, they were forgiven for what they had done the previous night. One of the thirteen attributes of God's mercy is long-suffering patience, but it does not last forever.

For one generation the glory of God was revealed to the entire world from Jerusalem. The Ark of the Covenant sat in its place in the Holy of Holies. The *Shechina* was in Zion.

But the permanence of the Temple and the continued Presence of the *Shechina* was conditional.

> God appeared to Solomon and said to him, "If you go before Me, as David your father went wholeheartedly and upright, to act in accord with all that I have commanded you and you will keep My statutes and laws, I will establish the throne of your kingdom over Israel forever as I have spoken to David your father, saying: A man will not fail you upon the throne of Israel. But if you and your children turn away from following Me and you will not observe My commandments and My statutes which I have placed before you, but go and worship other gods and bow down to them. Then I will cut Israel off from the land which I have given to them, and this House which I have sanctified to My Name I will dismiss from My Presence, and Israel shall be for a sign of disgrace among all nations."[110]

God had warned Israel not to mingle with the women of specific nations, *"for they will sway your heart after their gods," and to these did Solomon attach himself to love them.*[111]

"And it was at the time of Solomon's old age that his wives turned his heart after other gods and his heart was not whole with the Lord his God, like the heart of David, his father."[112]

Solomon built altars to the gods of his foreign wives, who offered incense and sacrifices to their deities.[113]

And God tore the kingdom away from Solomon, giving ten tribes to the northern kingdom of Israel, and leaving Solomon with two tribes, Judah

---

110. I Kings 9:4-7.

111. Ibid. 11:2.

112. Ibid. 11:2.

113. Ibid. 11:8.

and Benjamin. Eventually the tribe of Levi joined them, for the Temple was in Judea. For the sake of David, Solomon's father, God did not split the kingdom until the first year of the reign of Rehoboam, Solomon's son.

It is difficult to understand how King Solomon, the wisest man who ever lived,[114] could have made so great an error for which Israel has suffered for nearly three thousand years. From here we learn that wisdom and righteousness are two separate realms. David's bitterest and most wicked enemies were men of great wisdom: Achitofel, Doeg, Shimi ben Gera, and Absalom. As for David, his own righteousness stemmed not from wisdom, but from *devekut* (devotion) to God.

Then King Solomon was gathered to his fathers and was buried in the city of David. And his son, Rehoboam, sat on the throne of David.

Jeroboam, the newly anointed king of the northern tribes, was fearful that his subjects would visit the Temple in Jerusalem and be so impressed that they would rally to Rehoboam and assassinate Jeroboam. So he placed armed guards at every road leading to the Temple and blocked the people from traveling to Jerusalem, establishing his own religion based on the golden calf in Temples at Beth El and Dan.

For the better part of the next three hundred years, eighty per cent of the Jewish people were prevented from coming to the Temple. Both the Kingdom of Judea and the Kingdom of Israel were on a moral decline[115] that reached bottom when Manasseh, the fifteenth king of the Davidic dynasty, built an altar to alien gods in the Temple's courtyard and put an idol in the Holy of Holies to replace the Ark of the Covenant.

Manasseh's maniacal acts of terror in the name of his chosen pagan worship were legendary. He confiscated and destroyed every Torah scroll he could find and slaughtered hundreds of thousands of righteous Jews,

---

114. Ibid. 3:12.

115. Virtually all the kings of Israel were evil in the eyes of God. The situation in Judea was somewhat different as one righteous king gave way to a wicked king who gave way to another righteous king. But in the end the treachery of Judea was even worse than that of Israel and the decree of destruction was signed and sealed.

including his own maternal grandfather, the Prophet Isaiah.[116] The blood of the slain righteous flowed like a river through Jerusalem.

In the end, King Manasseh repented and returned to the God of his fathers, but it was too late to save the kingdom. His son and successor, Amon, tried to outdo Manasseh in wickedness and acts of defiance against God. Amon was assassinated after ruling for two years.

Some say that Manasseh put the idol in the Sanctuary, the chamber of the Menorah, and it was Amon who moved the idol into the Holy of Holies, replacing the Ark.

The Israelites worshipped many false gods during that period of time: the Asherah, the Baal, and Molech. The Asherah was a goddess who is identified as the queen of heaven, the goddess of fertility. The symbol of this deity was a tree. The Baal included a number of false gods worshipped in the region. This god was believed to be the source of material wealth. The third god of the pantheon of idols was Molech, an Ammonite god who was served by sacrificing one's own children to it, as it says (Leviticus 18:21), *"And you shall not give any of your offspring to Molech, nor shall you profane the Name of your God, I am the Lord."*

The *Molech* idol was made in the form of a bronze creature part human and part bull. In effect, it was an enormous furnace with a raging fire burning inside it. The priests of *Molech* would place a child on the idol's red hot hands and beat drums to drown out the screams of the child as it was burnt to death before the eyes of its parents.

We can see a remnant of Molech worship today as Muslims send their children to self-immolate in suicide bombings with the absurd belief that they will be rewarded in heaven for their barbaric stupidity. The *Gaon*, Rabbi Aaron Chaim Zimmerman, said, *"It is pure paganism to sacrifice a human being to Allah. If Islam can be construed to permit such sacrifice, then it is diametrically opposed to the ethical monotheism of Judaism. By this act they merely show how small they are and how small they have made their Creator."*[117]

After two years of his rule, King Amon was assassinated. His son Josiah, at the age of eight, became King of Judea. He immediately began searching

---

116. Babylonian Talmud, Yebamot 49b.

117. Torah and Reason, pp. 160-161.

for the God of Israel. By the age of twelve he had begun to purge the land of idol worship, as it says (2 Chron. 34:2), *"And he did that which was right in the eyes of the Lord and he walked in the ways of David his father, and turned aside neither to the right nor to the left."*

In the eighteenth year of his reign, King Josiah gave orders to refurbish the House of the Lord. During the process, the High Priest Hilkiah found the original book of Deuteronomy that was written by the hand of Moses.[118] It had been hidden out of fear that Manasseh or Amon would destroy it.

Shaphan the scribe read the words of the Law to King Josiah at the section where the scroll was found opened. And the verse read, *"The Lord will bring you and the king whom you will place over you unto a nation that you have not known, neither you nor your fathers, and there you will serve other gods, wood and stone."*[119]

King Josiah tore his garments in grief and sent Hilkiah, the High Priest and others to consult with Hulda, the prophetess, to understand the implication of finding the Torah open to those verses.

Hulda told them that it meant that God was going to bring total destruction upon Jerusalem and the Temple because the people had abandoned Him and served pagan deities. But because Josiah had humbled himself, he would not see the destruction, but would be gathered to his fathers in peace.

After hearing these words, Josiah launched a campaign to root every vestige of idol worship from the land. He removed the Asherah from the Temple and burnt it and destroyed all the utensils used for the worship of Baal. He defrocked the pagan priests and those who burnt incense to the sun and the moon and the constellations. He defiled the Molech idol so it could not be used for human sacrifice. He removed all the idolatrous temples that the kings of Israel had built and he executed the priests of idol worship in the northern kingdom, as it is written (2 Kings 23:25), *"Now, before him there was no king like him who returned to the Lord with all his heart and with all his soul and with all his possessions, according to the entire Torah of Moses and after him none arose."*

---

118. *Rashi* on II Chronicles 34:14.

119. *Rashi's* commentary to II Kings 22:13, referring to Deuteronomy 28:36,37.

Despite Josiah's efforts it was impossible to revoke the decree against Jerusalem and the Temple.

Finally, Josiah said to the Levites, *"Place the Holy Ark in the House that Solomon the son of David built."*[120]

These words from the Second Book of Chronicles are the last words written in Holy Scripture concerning the Ark of the Covenant. And ever since that day more than 2600 years ago, the Ark of the Covenant was never heard from nor seen.

Part Six – The Search for the Lost Ark

Is the Ark of the Covenant lost and gone forever? Or, is it merely hidden and waiting to be returned to the Holy of Holies of the Future Temple? And if it is hidden, where is it hidden?

Ever since Steven Spielberg created global awareness of the Ark with his movie, *Raiders of the Lost Ark,*[121] new theories and tales of discovery have been popping up like Greek soldiers from dragon's teeth. Practically every archaeologist and his uncle profess to know where the Ark is buried and several claim that they actually saw it. Invariably, these "Arkaeologists" fail to dig up the Lost Ark. And with passing time their triumphal claims of discovery seem to vanish.

From the Talmud[122]

It was said in the name of Rebbe Eliezer the Great: "The Ark went into exile with the Jewish people to Babylon."

Rebbe Eliezer maintained that the Ark was taken to Babylon when the Jews went into exile, and it is lost forever. He cites two verses to support his contention.

---

120. Despite Josiah's efforts it was impossible to revoke the decree against Jerusalem and the Temple.

121. Produced by Lucasfilm, Ltd., in 1981.

122. These discussions are found in the Jerusalem Talmud, Shekalim 15b and in the Babylonian Talmud, Yoma 53b.

The first verse is a prophecy told by Isaiah to King Hezekiah, *"Behold, a time will come when everything in your palace and all that your forefathers have stored up will be carried off to Babylon; no thing shall remain," says the Lord.*[123]

The Talmud explains that the *"thing"* of *"no thing shall remain"* refers to the Ark of the Covenant and the Tablets of the Ten Commandments contained within it. The Hebrew word here for *"thing"* is *davar,* which also means "saying" and is an allusion to the Ten Commandments.

Rebbe Eliezer's second proof text is the verse, *"And at the end of the year, King Nebuchadnezzar sent and brought [King Jehoiakim] to Babylon along with the precious vessels of the House of the Lord.*"[124]

Here, the Talmud states, *"What was the most precious vessel of the House of the Lord? The Ark!"*

From these two verses, according to Rebbe Eliezer, we see that Scripture tells us that the Ark was carried off by the Babylonian army and will never return.

The Talmud now offers an opposing view: *"The Rabbis say that the Ark was hidden away under the Temple in the Chamber of the Woodshed."* [125]

The Rabbis base their view on an interpretation of a verse in the Second Book of Chronicles. After King Josiah[126] heard the prophecy that Jerusalem was going to be destroyed, he issued the following order: *"And he [King Josiah] said to the Levites who taught all Israel and were holy to the Lord, 'Place the Holy Ark in the House that Solomon the son of*

---

123. II Kings 20:17, Isaiah 39:6.

124. II Chronicles 36:10.

125. The Chamber of the Woodshed was a chamber in the northeast corner of the Second Temple's Outer Courtyard (Women's Court). Wood that fueled the fires on the Great Sacrificial Altar was stored here.

126. King Josiah, a direct descendant of King David, ruled towards the end of the First Temple period as king of Judah from 3285 to 3315 (473-442 BCE/641-610 BCE).

David, the King of Israel, built; you will no longer have a burden on your shoulders; now serve the Lord your God and His people Israel.'"[127]

On this verse, *Rashi* comments:

> According to its simple meaning, the Levites were instructed to carry the Ark to the Holy of Holies of Solomon's Temple because Manasseh and Amon had removed the Holy Ark and replaced it with graven images, as is stated above concerning Manasseh: "He placed the graven image that he had made in the Temple of God."[128] Therefore, the pious King Josiah ordered that the Ark be returned to the chamber that Solomon had built for it [the Holy of Holies]. But our Rabbis said that, in fact, he commanded the Levites to hide it there [under the Temple].

The *Radak*[129] explains further:

> Josiah wished to spare the Ark the indignity of being carried away to the land of the enemy and so he hid it under the Temple. The Rabbis tell us that there was a stone in the western section of the Holy of Holies, upon which the Ark was placed. When Solomon built the Temple, he knew that it would ultimately be destroyed. Therefore, he built a secret hiding place for the Ark deep in the subterranean recesses of the Temple, which was covered by that stone. It was in this secret underground chamber that King Josiah ordered them to hide the Ark together with Aaron's staff, the flask of manna, and the anointing oil made by Moses.

---

127. II Chronicles 35:3.

128. Ibid. 33:7.

129. An acronym for Rabbi David Kimchi (1160-1235), who wrote one of the major commentaries on the Hebrew Scriptures.

The Talmud[130] brings a story to support the view of the Rabbis:

> An incident took place with a certain blemished *Kohen*[131] who was standing and splitting wood in the Chamber of the Woodshed. And he observed that one part of the stone flooring was different from the rest. He went to tell his co-worker, "Come and look at this part of the floor. It is different from the rest." But before he could finish the sentence, his soul departed. And they knew with certainty that the Ark was buried there.

Upon careful examination, the opinion of the Rabbis is anything but certain. The first problem is that the sudden death of a *Kohen* in the woodshed does not prove with certainty that the Ark was buried there. It could have had been a stroke that killed him, or a heart attack. The second problem is that the Chamber of the Woodshed, under which the Rabbis said that Solomon built his secret chamber, was 200 cubits (100 meters) from the Holy of Holies. Of course, one could argue that what the Rabbis meant was that there was a tunnel under the stone that led to the woodshed some 200 cubits away.

The third problem is that the woodshed mentioned in the Talmud was a Second Temple structure that did not exist at all in the First Temple (Solomon's Temple) when the Ark was hidden away.[132] Again, one could argue that the Rabbis meant that Solomon's secret chamber was built underneath the area where the Woodshed would stand in the Second Temple.

---

130. Shekalim 15b.

131. *Kohanim* with a physical defect that prevented them from participating in the sacrificial service were permitted to check the wood for the Altar to make sure there were no worms in it.

132. *Tzurath HaBayith* by *Tosefoth Yom Tov* explains that the woodshed in the Second Temple was a design element from Ezekiel's vision of the Messianic Temple. Ezekiel's prophecy was revealed after the First Temple was destroyed. So this woodshed did not exist in Solomon's Temple.

The fourth problem is that King Josiah reigned fifteen generations after King Solomon. If he had known the location of Solomon's secret underground chamber, he must have had a tradition dating back nearly four hundred years. But if that is so, why did they not return the Ark to the Second Temple which was built only seventy years after the First Temple was destroyed?

Since the primary purpose of the Holy Temple is to provide a house for the Ark,[133] why build a Temple that does not fulfill its purpose? There is only one plausible reason: the Ark was gone.

The fifth and final challenge to the Rabbis' view is that the verse states that King Josiah told the Levites that after they carried the Ark into *"the House the Solomon built,"* they would never have the burden of carrying it again. If he were asking them to carry it into the secret chamber under the Temple, then they would definitely have to carry it one more time when they would be privileged to move it back to its final resting place, the Holy of Holies. The only place King Josiah could have meant from which there would be no further carrying is the Holy of Holies itself, from which Nebuchadnezzar took it and carried it off to Babylon.

Based on all the above, it would appear that Rebbe Eliezer's opinion[134] is stronger than that of the Rabbis. Perhaps this is why it is written, *"If all the Sages of Israel were on one pan of a scale and Eliezer ben Hyrkanos were on the other, he would outweigh them all."*[135]

However, it should be realized that both opinions are based on interpretations of Biblical verses. When it comes to *halacha* (Jewish law) the interpretation of a verse can determine a final ruling. But when it comes to knowing the truth of history or nature, whatever happened happened and whatever is is, and no proof based on an interpretation of a verse can be considered conclusive.

Therefore, we are forced to say that the discussion in the Talmud leaves us with a doubt as to the location of the Ark. It may be hidden under the Temple Mount where the Woodshed stood in the Second Temple

---

133. Exodus 25:1, commentary of the *Ramban*.

134. that the Ark was carried away to Babylon and is gone forever.

135. *Pirkei Avoth* (Chapters of the Fathers) 2:12.

waiting to be retrieved by Elijah the Prophet or the Messiah and returned to the Holy of Holies of the Future Temple. Or, it may have been carried off to Babylon by Nebuchadnezzar and will never be seen again. Based on the Talmud, the choice is up to the individual as to which opinion he thinks is true.

The Prophecy of Jeremiah

Jeremiah was a *Kohen* (Jewish priest) who prophesied during the reign of the last five kings of Judea until the destruction of the First Temple.[136] He wrote four books of the Hebrew Scriptures: The First and Second Book of Kings, the Book of Jeremiah, and the Book of Lamentations.

Jeremiah was the chief of the prophets when King Josiah brought the Ark into the Holy of Holies of the First Temple,[137] or according to the Rabbis, to the secret chamber that King Solomon had built under the Temple Mount. Because Jeremiah was greater than that of the Talmudic sages[138] and because he was on the scene when the Ark disappeared, his view of the Ark's location is the most authoritative.

From the Book of Jeremiah, Chapter 3

Return, backsliding children, says the Lord, for I possessed you, and I will take you, one from a city and two from a family, and I will bring you to Zion.[139]

And it shall be, when you multiply and are fruitful in the land in those days, says the Lord, they will no longer say, "The Ark of the Covenant of the Lord," nor shall it come to mind, nor shall they mention it, nor shall they remember it, nor shall it be done anymore.[140]

---

136. From the Jewish year 3298 to 3338 (Circa 626 BCE to 586 BCE).

137. II Chronicles 35:3.

138. The prophet was a sage, but none of the sages were prophets.

139. Jeremiah 3:14.

140. Ibd. 3:16

Commentary: *"they will no longer say, 'The Ark of the Covenant of the Lord:'"* The Ark will be missing from the Second Temple and will be considered lost. Therefore, it will be forgotten. Another view is that the Ark will be missing from the Second Temple and also the Third Temple, which means that it will never return. *Rashi* comments that the entire congregation will be holy and the *Shechina* will dwell within the people as if they were the Ark.

These verses from the Book of Jeremiah leave us with a dilemma. If Jeremiah had been prophesying about the Messianic Era, then the Ark is lost and gone forever. But if his prophecy was about the Second Temple period, the fact that the Ark did not "come to mind nor was it mentioned" does not rule out its return in the future. The Second Temple stood for 420 years, all of them without the presence of the Ark, time enough for people to stop thinking or talking about it, and time enough to forget that the Ark is God's resting place on earth.

In either case, Jeremiah does not address the matter of the location of the Ark. For that, we have to look at the Second Book of Maccabees.

From the Second Book of Maccabees, 2:4 - 2:10

The Prophet Jeremiah, having been warned by God,[141] commanded that the Tabernacle and the Ark be taken with him as he went forth into the mountain where Moses had climbed up to see the heritage of God.[142]

---

141. God warned Jeremiah about the eventual destruction of the Temple and Jerusalem by the Babylonians.

142. This is Mount Nebo, from where God showed Moses the Holy Land and where Moses was buried. See Deuteronomy 34:1-5. The Torah tells us that the mountain is in Moab which today is Jordan, due east of Jericho and the Dead Sea.

When Jeremiah came there, he found a hollow cave wherein he laid the Tabernacle and the Ark and the Golden Incense Altar, and then he blocked the entrance.[143]

And some of those who had accompanied him left markers to show them the way back,[144] but they were unable to find the place.

When Jeremiah learned about what they had done, he chastised them, saying, "The place shall remain unknown until God shall gather His people together again and show mercy to them.

Then shall the Lord reveal these things to them and the glory of the Lord shall appear in a cloud as it was seen in the days of Moses and as when Solomon consecrated the Temple in order that it might receive the holiness that it deserves.

For it is written that he, being wise, offered sacrifices of dedication upon completion of the Temple.

And as when Moses prayed unto the Lord, the fire came down from heaven and consumed the sacrifices, so it was that when Solomon prayed, the fire came down from heaven, and consumed the burnt offerings.

As we can plainly see, the Second Book of Maccabees gives us the exact location of the Ark of the Covenant. It was hidden in a cave in Mount Nebo by the Prophet Jeremiah. It will remain there until the Final Redemption and the ingathering of the exiles. At that time, God will cause the Ark to return. This would appear to resolve all our questions and dilemmas.

---

143. With large stones that concealed the entrance to the cave.

144. So they could return and retrieve the Ark and the other objects.

There problem here is that the Rabbis reject the reliability of such apocryphal[145] texts as the Second Book of Maccabees. In the Mishnah,[146] Rabbi Akiva is quoted as having taught that one who reads "external books" has no share in the World to Come. While it is not explicitly known what Rabbi Akiva meant by "external books," the accepted view is that he was referring to quasi-canonical texts such as the Second Book of Maccabees. These books were not included in the Holy Scriptures and were considered not to have been written by prophecy or divine inspiration (*ruach hakodesh*).

Rabbi Menachem Meiri (1249-1301), in his commentary on the Talmud, wrote that Rabbi Akiva's prohibition against reading "external books" only concerns one who is seeking to follow their ways and depart from established Jewish tradition. But reading them merely to gain understanding is entirely permissible.

So what are we left with? Nothing carved in stone. It remains up to the individual to choose for himself. Many scholars believe that the Ark is hidden under the Temple Mount. Others say it is gone and lost forever.

The question remains: What action can any of this inspire in us? The Prophet Jeremiah declared that the Ark will be forgotten and, according to *Rashi* the people will become the Ark.[147] To accomplish this, we can learn the design of the Ark, its history and meaning, meditate on the place between the wings of the cherubim, and focus our energy on the two tablets of the Ten Commandments, the precious cargo of the Ark of the Covenant.

---

145. The Apocrypha or, more accurately the Pseudepigrapha, is Jewish extra-canonical Scripture written from around 200 B.C.E. to 200 C.E., and generally purported to be Holy Scripture, but whose authorship, with a few exceptions, is either unknown or falsely ascribed to men of great renown such as Daniel or Ezra. These books, such as the two books of Maccabees, certainly have ethical and spiritual value, but are said to stand outside the authentic tradition from Sinai.

146. Sanhedrin 10:1.

147. According to *Rashi's* commentary.

Numbers 10:35, 36

And it came to pass when the Ark would journey forth, Moses said, "Rise up, O Lord, and let Your enemies be scattered and let those who hate You flee before You." And when it returned, he said, "Rest, O Lord, among the myriad of thousands of Israel."

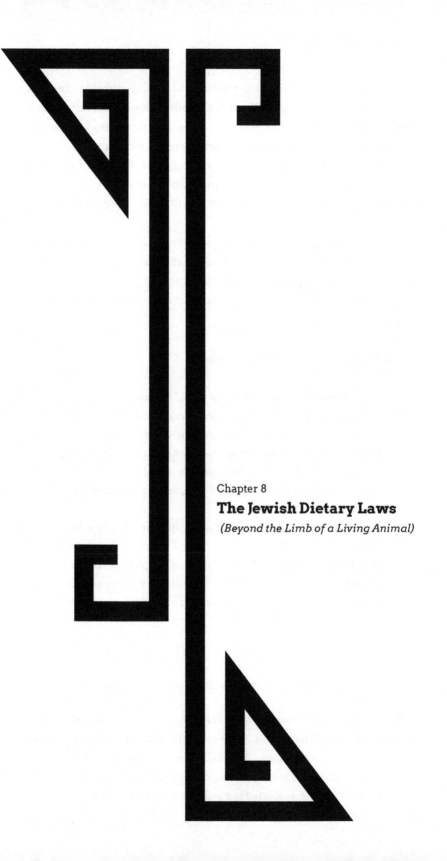

Chapter 8
The Jewish Dietary Laws
(Beyond the Limb of a Living Animal)

The prohibition against eating the limb of a living animal is one of the Seven Laws of the Children of Noah. For details of this commandment, see *The Path of the Righteous Gentile, Chapter Ten*. It is written there that the letter of the law serves only as a starting point which guarantees God's favor and ensures human morality. But if man wishes to actualize his intellectual and spiritual potential, he must tap into the "inner dimension" of the Noahide doctrine, through which he will realize the greatness of his soul.

Thus, not eating the limb of a living animal merely opens the portal to the refinement of intellect and emotion that man can attain through his eating habits and by practicing kindness to God's creatures. With this in mind, it is appropriate that *B'nai Noah* learn the basics of *Kashrut*, the Jewish Dietary Laws.

Part one: Correct Eating for All Mankind

It is written in the Ben Ish Chai,[1] *Genesis 3*

Since the sin of Adam and Chava (Eve) came through eating, the primary rectification of mankind will come through eating. This is similar to the principle of kashering pots and pans, or plates and cups, which had been rendered non-kosher by contact with forbidden food. The principle is: as it was absorbed, so will it be expelled.[2]

The soul of man absorbed *zuhama* (spiritual filth) by eating the forbidden fruit. Thus, the *zuhama* will be expelled by means of eating in a permissible, sanctified and spiritual manner. Therefore, the *yetzer hara* (evil inclination of man) and the satan and the *nachash* (primordial serpent) which are all one,

---

1. *Ben Ish Chai*, Genesis 3. Rabbi Yosef Chaim of Baghdad, 1832-1909.

2. Babylonian Talmud, Pesachim 30b. If forbidden food was absorbed into the walls of a pot through boiling, e.g., non-kosher chicken soup, the pot is scoured clean, then boiled out with water. The boiling water draws the contaminant out of the walls of the pot. If forbidden food was absorbed through a higher degree of heat, the pot is subjected to direct fire, a torch or burning coals. There are other ways of *kashering* utensils, but this is the general rule.

provoke and battle a person with matters of food consumption. And so, a person must purify and sanctify himself in the way he eats, for example, with *berachot* (blessings) recited with full attention, and by taking care that the food is unspoiled by forbidden substances such as worms or insects or blood or the presence of even a small amount of forbidden types of animals, birds and fish, or *nevelah*,[3] or *traifah*[4] or forbidden mixtures such as meat and milk. The food one eats cannot have been stolen or acquired dishonestly. Moreover, one should be careful to conduct himself with refinement at the table by saying words of Torah and avoiding slander or gluttony or drunkenness, or expressing anger or harsh strictness, for proper eating is the foundation of purification and holiness by which a person serves his Creator.

At the time of the Exodus from Egypt, the Children of Israel were commanded to sanctify themselves through eating, as it says (Exodus 12:8), *"And this night they shall eat the meat of the Passover lamb, roasted by fire, with matzot and maror (bitter herbs) shall they eat it."*

The Israelites continued to eat matzah[5] for the entire Passover holiday as they wandered into the Wilderness, as it says (Exodus 12:15), *"Seven days shall you eat matzah, and from the first day you shall have removed all leavened food from your houses, for whoever eats anything leavened[6]*

---

3. Animals or birds that died of themselves or were improperly slaughtered.

4. Animals or birds that were sick or wounded in a manner that rendered them non-kosher.

5. Matzah is made solely of flour and water, kneaded and rolled thin, then baked before it has time to rise. It is the humble bread eaten by the poor and has become known as the bread of faith.

6. The Hebrew word for leavening is *chametz*, meaning sour, a word closely related to *chometz*, vinegar. It is the souring agent that causes bread to rise and be classified as *chametz*, a process that is said to take 18 minutes. Matzah is flour that is kneaded and baked in less time than 18 minutes, thus pre-empting the process of its becoming *chametz*.

from the first day until the seventh day, that soul shall be cut off from Israel."

Adam had been commanded not to eat the fruit of the Tree of Knowledge of Good and Evil. Noah had been commanded not to eat the limb of a living animal.[7] But the preparation for leaving Egypt included the first time that God issued a positive commandment to eat a specific food as a service to Him. Eating matzah was the first phase of a two-phase rectification of eating the forbidden fruit.

The matzah that the Jews brought with them from Egypt lasted for a month and then it ran out. The next morning, phase two of the rectification began. Manna fell from heaven.

Manna was miraculous, celestial, perfect food. It had just enough substance to prevent it from floating back up to heaven, but no more than that, as it says (Exodus 16:14), *"And in the morning there was a layer of dew around the camp. And when the dew evaporated, behold, upon the face of the wilderness a fine flaky substance, fine like frost upon the ground."*

Manna is described as tiny round pellets like coriander seed, but white in color, and tasting like wafers made with honey. Each person ate an *omer* of manna every day. This is estimated at 2.1 liters or 2.2 quarts of manna per day.

Manna produced no excrement or bodily waste of any kind. For nineteen days the people ate manna,[8] purifying and sanctifying their bodies with this food from heaven. By the twentieth day, the *zuhama* had been completely expelled. All the people had been healed of every ailment and wound. The blind could see and the lame could walk upright. They had been raised above the sin of eating from the Tree of Knowledge of good and evil. Death had no hold upon them.

---

7. Genesis 9:3-4, *"Every moving thing that lives, shall be food for you; as the green herbs, I have given you everything. But the flesh with its life, its blood, you shall not eat."*

8. From the 16th day of the Hebrew month of Iyar until the 5th day of Sivan, the day before God said the Ten Commandments. 19 is the numerical value of Chava (Eve).

On that day, they heard the voice of God speak the Ten Commandments from atop Mount Sinai. They had become a holy people and a nation of priests who were destined to live forever.

The next morning, Moses ascended Mount Sinai to receive the Tablets of the Ten Commandments, which would seal the covenant between God and Israel. According to the *Zohar*, these Tablets of the Covenant were written by the finger of God on stone tablets of divine origin. They were from the *Etz Chaim*, the Tree of Life. Had the First Tablets been received and accepted, the Children of Israel would have lived forever. But with Moses out of sight, the recently liberated slaves lost their way and worshipped the golden calf, and the Tablets of the Covenant were broken.

Moses pleaded with God to forgive the people, and He did. But the Children of Israel had forfeited the gift of ultimate purity and sanctity and the *zuhama* once more began to flow through their bodies. Even though they would continue to eat manna for forty years in the wilderness, they were mortal once more. Thus began the slow march towards the Final Redemption and the coming of Messiah when the *zuhama* would be banished forever, as it says (Zechariah 13:1-2), *"On that day, a spring will be opened for the House of David and for the inhabitants of Jerusalem, for cleansing and for purification ... and the spirit of impurity I will remove from the earth."*

In the meantime, two new tablets had been carved out of the earth by Moses and carried up to the top of Mount Sinai. The finger of God wrote upon them the same words as had been written on the First Tablets, which were the words of the Ten Commandments that God had spoken to all the people.

The *Zohar*[9] tells us that the second tablets were a consolation. The words were still from the Tree of Life, but now they were filtered through the *Etz HaDaat*, the Tree of Knowledge. We now had to settle for the knowledge of how to choose good and reject evil. This included the knowledge of how to eat correctly so as to remain physically and spiritually healthy and prolong our lives and the lives of our children.

Optimum Health

---

9. Zohar, Bereshit 26b.

The Jewish dietary laws guarantee physical and spiritual well-being throughout a person's life. One who is sick or in physical pain cannot properly serve God or care for his own soul. This is especially so if the person is, God forbid, chronically ill or has suffered long-term pain. Therefore, maintaining excellent health is an integral part of the Jewish dietary laws.

Eight hundred years ago, the *Rambam*[10] laid down basic principles of diet in relationship to healthy living that are cutting edge wisdom even today.

Adapted from the Mishneh Torah [11]

The general principle is that a person should be moderate in all matters until he reaches and maintains the middle path.[12] This is what King Solomon meant when he wrote, *"Measure the path of your feet and all your ways will be established (Proverbs 4:26)."*

A person might say, "Since envy, lust, and honor are wrong pursuits that destroy a person from the world, I will separate from them and follow the opposite extreme. I will not eat meat nor drink wine, nor marry a woman, nor live in a fine house. And I will not wear fine clothing. Rather I will wear sackcloth and coarse wool and conduct my life the way priests of some foreign religions do."

---

10. An acrostic for Rabbi Moshe ben Maimon (1135-1204), the great Talmudic scholar, philosopher, and physician.

11. The *Mishneh Torah* is the magnum opus of the *Rambam* These selections were taken from the *Mishneh Torah*, Book of Knowledge, Rules of Conduct, chapters 3, 4 and 5.

12. The middle path is the path of power upon which one is most likely to succeed in all endeavors.

This is a wrong path and it is forbidden to walk it. Whoever travels this path is considered a sinner, as it says about a Nazirite,[13] "If a Nazirite who merely abstained from wine requires a sin-offering, then a person who abstains from everything certainly requires it. Are the prohibitions of the Torah not enough for you that you withhold yourself from permitted things?"

This general rule includes a person who starves himself through frequent fasting. About extreme asceticism, King Solomon wrote (Ecclesiastes 7:16), *Do not be too righteous or overly wise; why make yourself desolate?*[14]

Rather, a person should focus his heart and actions upon increasing his awareness of God. And this should determine the way he lies down, arises and speaks. Similarly, he should not eat and drink for mere physical pleasure, but in order to maintain a healthy body. Therefore, he should not eat to satisfy his cravings like a dog or a donkey, but eat food that is beneficial for bodily health, whether the food is bitter or sweet.

A person should stay away from food that is delicious but harmful. For example, one with a hot temperament should not eat meat or sugar, nor should he drink wine, as King Solomon warned (Proverbs 25:27), *"Eating too much honey*[15] *is not good; rather search for the honor of those things that deserve honor."* Instead, he should drink endive juice even though it tastes bitter, and eat and drink only for nutritional value in order to be healthy and whole, since it is impossible for a person to live without eating and drinking.

However, even if a person follows the rules of medical wisdom, but does so merely to attain a healthy body for its own sake, he is on the

---

13. A Nazirite abstains from drinking wine, cutting his hair, and any contact with a dead person for a stipulated period of time. After the Nazirite finishes this stipulated time, he brings several offerings to the Holy Temple, including a sin offering, as we learn in Number 6:14.

14. An ascetic fails to fulfill his potential and contributes little or nothing to the society.

15. When scripture uses the term honey, it means cane sugar or date or fig honey.

wrong path. Rather, he should build the body whole and strong so that his soul is upright and able to know God, for it is impossible to meditate or contemplate wisdom if one is starving or sick or suffering with pain.

Concerning this, our sages have said, "*Let all your deeds be for the sake of Heaven.*"[16] And King Solomon stated in his wisdom (Proverbs 3:6), "*In all your ways know Him and He will straighten your paths.*"

Maintaining a body that is healthy and whole is an aspect of the way of God, for a person cannot understand or know any knowledge of the Creator if he is sick. Therefore a person must distance himself from things that damage the body and become accustomed to a healthy way of eating.

1. One should not eat so much that he completely fills his stomach, but should stop when he feels about three quarters' full.

2. He should not drink water during the meal, except perhaps a small amount, and this should be mixed with wine.[17] When the food has begun the digestive process, one may drink what he needs, but one should never drink large volumes of water, even after the food is completely digested.

3. One should not eat before he has clearly determined whether or not he needs to relieve himself. And if he feels the slightest urge, he should act upon it.

4. One should not eat until after he has taken a stroll to warm up his body or has done some kind of physical exercise to warm his body, particularly in the morning. Then he should rest for a bit to settle his body, and then eat. Bathing his body in hot water after exercising is good, after which he should drink a little and then eat.

5. A person should always eat while sitting or leaning to his left side. He should not eat while walking or riding [a horse] or while exercising or when the body is stressed. He should not go for a walk until his food is at

---

16. Chapters of the Fathers 2:15. God is sometimes referred to as Heaven in rabbinic literature.

17. It is possible that the water in the middle east during the beginning of the 13th century was not pure as it is not pure in many parts of the world today, which is one of the reasons why tea is the drink of the orient – because boiled water is safer to drink. Also, today red wine drunk in moderation is seen by nutritionists as extremely beneficial to the arterial system of the body.

least partially digested. Anyone who takes a walk or exercises strenuously right after eating does serious damage to himself.

6. A person should not go to sleep for the night immediately after eating, but should wait three or four hours. And he should not make the daylight hours the time when he sleeps.[18]

7. Foods that loosen the bowels, such as grapes, figs, mulberries, pears, melons, peeled cucumbers or the like should be eaten as an appetizer to the meal. He should wait briefly until these foods have left the upper stomach, and then eat his meal.

8. Foods that are binding, such as pomegranates, quinces, and apples should be eaten sparingly after the meal.

9. A person who chooses to eat both poultry and red meat at a single meal should eat the poultry first. Similarly, if he eats eggs and poultry, he should eat the eggs first. And red meat from smaller animals [e.g. lamb] should be eaten before that of larger animals (beef). As a rule, lighter food should precede heavier food.[19]

10. During the summer, one should eat cold foods that are lightly spiced and use vinegar. In the rainy season, eat hot food that is highly spiced, and mustard and asafetida.[20] This approach is applicable to places with cold or hot climates, adjusting the diet to fit the climate.

11. There are foods that are extremely harmful and should never be eaten, for example, large fish that are salted and aged,[21] aged salty cheese, aged salty meat, wine straight from the press, cooked food that has been

---

18. This does not negate the value of taking a nap during the day.

19. The question of eating meat will be discussed later. Suffice it to say here that Jewish tradition definitely includes eating meat as is evident here from the *Rambam*.

20. A flavorful plant indigenous to India. It is anti-flatulent and aids digestion. It has a strong flavor and is preferably used only when cooked. It is likely that onions, leek, and garlic would be recommended here.

21. It is possible that fish were salted as a preservative in the *Rambam's* time.

sitting around and smells bad[22] or has begun to taste bitter.[23] These are all like poisons to the body.[24]

12. There are other foods that are less harmful than those on the previous list, but are still not recommended except when eaten in small amounts and infrequently. These are large fish,[25] fresh cheese and other milk products that have been standing around for more than 24 hours, tough meat of oxen and he-goats, fava beans, barley bread, and matza.[26]

13. There are foods which are still harmful, but less than these, such as water fowl, young pigeons, dates, bread fried in oil or kneaded with

---

22. The rule of thumb is that if you have the slightest doubt about the safety of the food, get rid of it. Rather err by disposing food too soon than get food poisoning.

23. This means a bad or bitter taste resulting from food that has become spoiled, rather than a food whose actual taste is bitter like curly endive or dandelion greens.

24. We have omitted mushrooms which the Rambam included in this list. We presume mushrooms were included because, in his days, they were mostly collected in wild and several common varieties are poisonous. Modern nutritionists include mushrooms among the healthiest of foods, particularly oriental varieties such as the shitake mushroom.

25. Some large fish are healthy. Others are dangerous because they are at the end of the aquatic food chain. Today, many large fish are actually poisonous because of the toxic waste that is found in them.

26. The *Rambam* apparently wants us to avoid matza as regular fare because it is made of white flour and can sit around for months which can be problematic. He rejects several vegetables that nutritionists consider quite healthy – lentils, chick peas, cabbage, leeks, onions, garlic, and radishes. We have omitted his inclusion of these. The *Rambam* derived most of the foods on this list from the Talmud, and we know that the nature of many vegetables has changed since Talmudic times (1500-2000 years ago). For example, the Talmud tells us that carrots are so woody that it is impossible to eat one raw.

oil, highly processed flour, gravy or fish brine.[27] These should be eaten sparingly. One who is wise and controls his cravings and avoids these foods unless he has a medical reason for eating them, is a mighty soul.

14. One should not eat a lot of fruit, even when dried and especially when fresh. Under ripe fruit are like swords to the body. Carob is always bad.[28] Fruit that is preserved by pickling is problematic and should be eaten sparingly and only in the summer and in hot climates. Figs, grapes, and almonds are always good, whether fresh or dried, and a person can eat as much of them as he wants, but he should not snack on them constantly despite their being the best of all fruit.

15. Honey[29] and wine are damaging to children and healthy for the elderly. This applies particularly in the rainy season. As a rule, in the summer one should eat two-thirds of what he eats in the winter.

16. A person should always try to have loose bowels, even tending slightly towards diarrhea. This is a basic principle of good health: constipation and hard bowel movements will bring serious illness upon a person. What can one do to alleviate constipation? He should eat dark rich greens, such as spinach, well-cooked and seasoned with olive oil. If he is elderly, he can drink honey in hot water in the morning and wait four hours before he has breakfast and do this every day until the situation improves.

17. The sages have taught another basic principle for good health: So long as a person exercises with effort and does not overeat and his bowels are loose, he will not become ill and will grow strong, even if he eats harmful food. But anyone who is sedentary and does not exercise or holds back going to the bathroom when he feels the urge, or is regularly

---

27. It would seem that the characteristic these foods share in common is richness. Waterfowl, ducks and geese are extremely fatty, as are young pigeons, etc. And today we know that sugar, processed white flour and rich gravies are damaging to the arterial system.

28. It turns out that, according to contemporary thought, carob has many health benefits. It is, however, constipating which the *Rambam* considers extremely problematic.

29. This apparently refers to bee honey which can be dangerous for babies and toddlers.

constipated, even if he eats good food and takes care of himself from a nutritional perspective, will constantly suffer pain and will grow weaker.

18. Overeating is like poison to the body and is the main cause of all sickness. The majority of illnesses come to a person from eating harmful food or overeating, even if the food is healthful. It is as King Solomon said in his wisdom (Proverbs 21:23), *"A person who guards his mouth and his tongue, guards his soul from suffering."* This means he guards his mouth from eating harmful food or overeating, and guards his tongue from speaking unnecessary words.

✻ ✻ ✻ ✻

The 32 Healtiest Foods

A consensus of contemporary nutritionists lists the following as the 32 healthiest foods: Almonds, apples, avocados, bananas, beets, black beans, blueberries, whole wheat bread, broccoli, brussel sprouts, bulgar, chia seeds, dark chocolate, eggplant, flax seeds, kale, kidney beans, lentils, lean red meat, fat-free milk, steel-cut oatmeal, extra virgin olive oil, pumpkin, quinoa, wild salmon, spinach, sweet potatoes, tomatoes, tuna, walnuts, red wine, fat-free yogurt. Many nutritionists put green tea, particularly if it has a little lemon juice added, at the very top of the list.

If a person makes these the majority of the food he eats, follows the guidelines of the *Rambam*, does not overeat, and exercises regularly (a 30-minute brisk walk four or more times a week is sufficient), he will remain healthy for the rest of his life.[30]

Reasons for the Dietary Laws

While optimum health is a benefit of the dietary laws, it is not the primary reason they were given to us.

---

30. The *Rambam* adds the disclaimer: unless the person had already damaged himself.

In his allegorical writings, Philo[31] maintained that the dietary laws were given to awaken pious thoughts, raise consciousness, and refine a person's character.

By following the Jewish dietary laws, a person is given the tools to take control of his animal nature. He is gently but continuously reminded that there is a spiritual aspect to every physical act of eating.

In the end, it is the Torah itself that gives us the primary reason for the Jewish dietary laws. After delineating which animals, fish and insects are kosher and which are not, God says (Leviticus 11:44), *"For I am the Lord your God; sanctify yourselves and be holy, for I am holy."*

The Torah tells us to sanctify ourselves and become holy because God is holy and He wants us to emulate Him as best as we can, as it says (Proverbs 3:6), *"Know Him in all your ways and He will straighten your paths."* For this purpose, we have been given the Jewish dietary laws. Once attuned to this way of eating, a person becomes a kosher vessel for the Godly Light, as it says (Psalms 82:6), *"I said you are angels and all of you are children of the Most High."*

Keeping Kosher: The Basics

Correct eating is indispensable to success in personal refinement. From a Jewish perspective, it is impossible to eat correctly without keeping kosher.

Keeping kosher can be simple or complex. A person can follow a few basic principles and be done with it. Or, he can make the study and observance of the Torah's dietary laws a lifelong pursuit. Since this book is written primarily for the edification of Noahides, we will limit our discussion to a few practical basics of keeping kosher.

The Jewish dietary laws which have become known as "keeping kosher" are a set of Biblical commandments that were later amended and expanded by Talmudic and rabbinic decrees.

---

31. Philo of Alexandria 20 BCE – 50 CE, a Jewish philosopher and nobleman who spoke on behalf of the Alexandrian community at the Roman court of Caligula.

Some Basic Terms

kosher: fit or acceptable. Applied to food, it indicates that a food is acceptable according to Jewish dietary law.

kashrut: the status of food as kosher or non-kosher. A *kashrut* organization certifies that certain products are kosher.

hechsher: the rabbinic certification that a product is kosher.

trefa or traif: the term used to describe food that is not kosher.[32] The word actually means torn, referring to an animal that has been damaged in a way that renders it unfit, such as having a punctured lung. Forbidden types of animals, birds, or fish are also categorized as *traif.*

nevelah: an animal or bird that died in a manner rendering it unfit, such as by improper slaughtering or sickness or simply old age. The term is normally used with reference to kosher species of animals.

kosher-style: certain kinds of traditional Jewish foods, such as kosher style corned beef or salami. The term has no relationship to Jewish dietary laws. In fact, when you see the term kosher-style, particularly on a restaurant, it generally means that the food is *traif.* There are exceptions. Kosher-style pickles could actually be kosher.

glatt kosher: a high level of *kashrut. Glatt* is a Yiddish word meaning smooth, indicating that the lungs of a slaughtered animal were found to be free of lesions. Sefardic Jews use the term halak, the Hebrew word for smooth.

Parve: food that is neither meat nor milk. Vegetables, fruit, grains are examples of parve food.

Kosher Animals

The Torah gives us clear guidelines as to which animals may be eaten. *"You shall not eat any abomination. These are the animals that you may eat: the ox, sheep and goat; hart and deer and yachmur and akko and*

---

32. The real term is *trefa,* but no one seems to use it. If you say something is *trefa,* very few English-speaking people will know what you mean.

dishon and tio and zamer.[33] *And every animal that has a split hoof which is entirely separated as two hooves and that chews its cud among the animals – it you may eat (Deuteronomy 14:3-6)."*

If an animal chews its cud but does not have split hooves, like the camel, it is forbidden. Or if it has split hooves but does not chew its cud, like the pig, it is also forbidden. To be a kosher species, the animal must have both signs. All other animals are unclean and forbidden.[34]

It should be noted that none of the animals designated as kosher are predators.

Practically speaking, the only kosher red meat that is commercially available is beef and lamb and, rarely, goat (kid).[35]

In order to be kosher, an animal requires *shechita* (ritually correct slaughtering). A razor-sharp knife is used by a highly-skilled *shochet* to sever the esophagus and windpipe. If the knife has the slightest nick in the blade, the *shechita* is not kosher. *Shechita* is the most humane form of slaughter. The animal does not feel the razor sharp blade and the blood rushes from the brain rendering it unconscious instantly. There is literally no suffering other than the stress and agitation of being led to the slaughter.

After the animal is slaughtered, its insides are checked for signs that would render it *traif.*

The sciatic nerve is removed.[36] Also, certain fats called *chelev* are removed.

---

33. All the obscure or untranslated species are in either the cattle or deer or antelope families.

34. Unclean does not mean they are evil or unworthy, merely that they may not be eaten.

35. If you can find some giraffe pot roast, go for it, and send us the recipe.

36. This is called *nikkur* or, in Yiddish, *trayber.* Doing it correctly requires skill. To avoid problems, the prevailing custom (at least among Ashkenazim) is to use meat only from the forequarters since the sciatic nerve is found in the hind quarters. In Israel today, more butchers are willing to *trayber* than outside the land.

Finally, the blood is removed by soaking and salting the meat or roasting it over an open flame. Today, most commercially sold kosher meat has the blood removed by the processing plant or the butcher. But some packaged meat is still sold that relies on the purchaser to do the *kashering*. Packaged meat that has been soaked and salted is labeled as *muchshar* (*kashered*).

Kosher Birds

The Torah tells us that we may eat any species of bird that is *tahor* (spiritual clean). It then names twenty-four species that are not to be eaten – from the vulture to the bat.[37] Presumably, all the other species of birds are kosher.

However, because of the exile and dispersion to all parts of the world, we have lost the precise knowledge of many of the unclean or clean species of birds. Therefore, it is the prevailing custom to eat only birds with a well-established tradition of being kosher. The accepted kosher fowl are chicken, pigeon, dove, domestic duck, domestic goose, pheasant and quail. The turkey is the only species of bird that is accepted as kosher without a clear tradition. For this reason, there are some observant Jews who will not eat turkey.

None of the kosher species of birds are predators, although chickens come close. Just watch what happens if a mouse wanders into a hen house!

Birds must be ritually slaughtered. The feathers and insides are then removed and the blood is drained by soaking and salting or roasting over an open flame.

Kosher Fish

The Torah gives us signs for determining which fish are kosher. "These *you may eat of all that are in the waters: whatever has fins and scales in the waters, in the seas and in the rivers, these you may eat (Leviticus 11:9)."*

---

37. The names of the unclean birds are given in two places in the Torah, Leviticus 11:13-18 and Deuteronomy 14:11-20.

Most species of commercially sold fish have fins and scales, but a few do not. The catfish has no scales and is, therefore, *traif*. Shellfish such as lobster, shrimp, clams, oysters, crabs and scallops are not kosher. For a fish to be kosher, the scales must be the kind that is easily removed. Sturgeon is not kosher because it has armor-plated scales that are permanently attached to the skin. This means that true caviar, which is sturgeon roe, is not kosher.

Fish do not require ritual slaughtering and fish blood may be eaten.

Kosher Insects

All insects are traif with the following exception: *"Only this may you eat from among the flying swarming creatures that walk on four legs – one that has jointed legs above its feet with which they leap upon the earth. You may eat these from among them: the arbeh according to its kind, the sal'am according to its kind, the chargol according to its kind, and the chagav according to its kind (Leviticus 11:21,22)."*

These mentioned creatures are four types of locusts. The Yemenite Jews have a tradition of which are the permissible ones. Therefore, these species of locusts are kosher for Yemenite Jews.[38] According to Yemenite tradition, the *arbeh* is the red locust, the *sal'am* is the yellow locust, the *chargol* is the spotted gray locust, and the *chagav* is the white locust. How do these locusts taste? Well, no kosher food tastes bad, so locusts are probably no exception.[39] Ask a Yemenite.

Blood

The Torah permits us to eat animal flesh, but Israelites are forbidden to eat blood and are required to treat the blood of a slaughtered animal with respect.

---

38. People who are guests of Yemenite Jews are permitted to rely on their tradition. So the next time you visit Yemen, do not fail to miss this great culinary delight.

39. The Chinese people dry roast locusts and eat them as snacks like peanuts.

Eating blood defiles the soul even more than eating pork. One of the directives given to Noah after the Flood, says, (Genesis 9:4), *"But flesh with its life, which is its blood, you shall not eat."* This is not a prohibition of eating blood, but of eating animal flesh while the animal is alive, i.e., *aiver min hachai* (the limb of a living animal). The way the commandment is worded demonstrates the close relationship between an animal's life force and its blood.

At Mount Sinai it was stated with stronger language (Deuteronomy 12:23), *"Be careful that you do not eat the blood, for the blood is the life and you shall not eat the life with the flesh."*

Out of respect for the sanctity of life, when fowl or kosher animals[40] are slaughtered, their blood is covered with earth, as it says (Leviticus 17:13), *"And he shall pour out its blood, and cover it with earth."*

Rabbenu Bachye offers a philosophical reason for the prohibition of eating blood: *Blood represents animal life and it is improper for us to mix that nature with our nature. We were commanded to make our nature gentle and merciful, not cruel. If we ate blood our souls would give rise to cruelty or coarseness of nature like the beastly soul.*[41]

We are instructed to make a distinction between animals that devour their prey with its blood, and man who is supposed to be gentle and merciful. Therefore, we take care that the soul of man is not defiled by consuming animal blood.

---

40. This refers specifically to non-domesticated animals, such as deer and antelope.

41. Commentary to Leviticus 16:11. Bachye ben Asher, known as Rabbenu Bachye (circa 1250-1340), wrote a commentary on the Hebrew Scriptures and is noted for introducing Kabbalah into Torah study.

Fruit and vegetables

All fruit and vegetables are essentially kosher.[42] But one must carefully check whether the produce contains worms, weevils, mites, thrips, moth larvae, small flies and countless other creepy crawlies that love fruit and vegetables as much as we do. Bug infestation is a common problem with fruit, nuts, grains, beans, and vegetables of all kinds. Anyone who keeps kosher is obligated to inspect fruit and vegetables before eating them.

Eating insects, even inadvertently, is a serious problem, for it says (Leviticus 11:43), *"Do not make your souls detestable by eating swarming creatures and do not defile yourself with them and become unclean through them."*

Not all food items need checking. Some are known to be clean. Apples, bananas, oranges,[43] for example, are generally clean and do not require checking except for that occasional worm in an apple.[44] Dried figs and dates, on the other hand, must be opened one by one and checked very carefully because tiny worms, beetles or mites are commonly found inside them. Rice, barley, and other grains require checking, particularly if they have been stored for a long time. Leafy vegetables may have tiny insects on them that are the same color as the leaves.

What complicates matters is that the situation with various types of fruit or vegetables or grains can change from season to season and locale to locale.

A friend of ours told us about an experience he had when he spent a year in Chicago, where the Orthodox Rabbis had officially ruled that commercially packaged flour was bug-free and did not require checking.

---

42. Fruit and vegetable grown inside the land of Israel have a number of restrictions, such as obligatory tithes and produce of the Sabbatical Year. These issues are beyond the parameters of this book. Any comprehensive treatise on *kashrut* will include these matters and an internet search will reveal the pertinent information as well.

43. A tiny insect called "scale" is often found on orange peels.

44. The joke goes: What's worse than finding a worm in an apple? Finding half a worm in an apple.

This friend and his wife had just come to Chicago from Los Angeles, where the custom was to check flour for bugs and worms by sifting it with a fine sifter. My friend's wife simply continued her normal routine, even in Chicago. Every Friday morning before she baked the challah for Shabbat, she would sift the flour and every week she would find a few small golden worms left behind in the sifter. When she reported this during a class she was taking, the rabbi giving the class, who was one of Chicago's leading experts in *kashrut*, nearly fainted. The situation with packaged flour had changed, and no one knew about it.

Checking for bugs can be a daunting procedure, ranging from a careful visual inspection of rice and other grains to rinsing vegetables vigorously with running water to soaking them in a solution of diluted vinegar and checking to see if any bugs were left behind in the tub.

In one regard, eating insects is even worse than eating *traif* meat. When someone eats a bug, the person generally eats the entire creature, whereas with *traif* meat, only a small bit of the forbidden creature is consumed. Someone who eats buggy strawberries or romaine lettuce or other infested fruit and vegetables can consume many insects at one sitting.

Separation of Meat and Milk

In three separate verses,[45] the Torah tells us *not to boil a kid in its mother's milk*. This was interpreted by the sages to include three separate prohibitions:

1. Not to cook meat and dairy products together.

2. Not to eat meat and dairy products which were cooked together.

3. Not to benefit from meat and dairy products which were cooked together (such as feeding them to one's pets).

Later, the Rabbis amended and extended these three prohibitions to include eating meat and dairy products together even if they were not

---

45. Exodus 23:19, Exodus 34:26, Deuteronomy 14:21.

cooked together. And then they further amended it to include poultry.[46] And then once more they amended it to require waiting up to six hours between eating meat and dairy products.

Today, a strictly kosher household will have at least two sets of pots and pans, one for meat and one for dairy, plus two sets of dishes and cutlery, two ovens and often two dishwashers, and some have two sets of kitchen towels and tablecloths.[47]

Consider this: If an Orthodox Jewish housewife tastes a spoonful of chicken soup, she may not take a sip of milk for six full hours. Is this mass hysteria? What is going on here?

The fact is boiling a kid in its mother's milk is not really about cooking or eating meat and milk together. It is about idol worship. That is the reason for the seemingly obsessive behavior.

The act of boiling a kid in its mother's milk was a fertility rite of the ancient Canaanites[48] who believed that their gods controlled the reproduction of man and beast and grain. To gain favor from the gods, the Canaanites performed this pagan sacrifice at the harvest season. Therefore, the Torah prohibited boiling a kid in its mother's milk three separate times to keep the Jewish people far away from such idolatrous rituals.

The result was that, for the Jew, mixing meat and milk became the chief symbol of pagan brutality and idol worship.[49] What could be more

---

46. Even though, to the best of our knowledge, chickens do not give milk. Therefore, it is unlikely that one could boil a baby chick in mama hen's milk. Forbidding poultry with dairy is a fence to protect you from eating red meat with dairy.

47. Some people have a third set for *parve*, i.e., foods that are neither meat or dairy. And, of course, on Passover everyone has two additional sets of everything. It has become so complicated that many Orthodox Jews eat exclusively or largely on disposable plasticware.

48. Larousse Encyclopedia of Mythology, pp. 77-79.

49. Had the Torah had been given in this millennium, separating wafers and wine might well have replaced meat and milk as the chief symbols of pagan idolatry.

perverse than killing a mother and her baby and cooking the baby in the very milk intended to nourish it?

So when it comes to keeping kosher, cheeseburgers, pepperoni pizza, beef stroganoff, and chicken Kiev are strictly off limits.

The question is: how exacting should one be when it comes to separating meat and milk?

Abraham was the first Patriarch of the Jews and the *Gerim*. All the families of the world are blessed through him. He was a spiritual giant who received God's unqualified approval. The oral tradition teaches that Abraham kept the entire Torah even before it was given on Mount Sinai. And yet, we see that Abraham served meat and milk at the same meal, as it says (Genesis 18:8), *"And he took butter and milk and the veal that he had prepared and set it before them."* No Orthodox Rabbi would permit that today.

Placing chicken and other poultry in the category of red meat was unknown until the time of the *Mishna*.[50] And the practice of waiting an extended period of time between meat and dairy meals originated several hundred years after that.

Concerning the practice of waiting between one meal and the next,[51] there are four basic customs. The prevalent custom is to wait six hours.[52] German Jews wait three hours. Jews from the Netherlands wait one hour. The *Baalei Tosefot*[53] held that a person could finish a meat meal, say grace after meals, and then start the dairy meal without waiting at all.

---

50. Circa 180 CE, approximately 1500 years after the giving of the Torah on Mount Sinai.

51. Waiting between meals is necessary only if the meat meal is first. If the dairy meal is first, rinsing one's mouth in between is sufficient unless one ate hard cheese, like Emmenthal Swiss or some aged cheddar cheeses. It is worth noting that Abraham served the butter and milk before the meat.

52. According to the *Rambam*, this is the time it takes for meat stuck between your teeth to become nullified.

53. The *Baalei Tosafot* were Talmudic scholars in France and Germany during the 12th and 13th centuries.

Since separation of meat and milk is one of the most distinctive aspects of the Jewish dietary laws, anyone who keeps kosher is well-advised to take it seriously. How seriously depends on the sensibility of the individual. Most of all, a God fearing person should remain mindful of the fact that separating meat and milk is really about rejecting idolatry. It is easy to lose sight of this and to separate meat and milk mechanically, without awareness of any spiritual meaning.

The daily activities of eating and drinking can elevate a person or lower him. The human being can eat like a dog or like a human being made in the image of God. The refinement that results from keeping kosher shows on body and soul, on the bones, the sinews, the flesh, the skin and the bone marrow. It affects a person's thoughts, speech, and deeds and determines the degree of Godly light that emanates from within him or her.

The essence of the Torah is to take that which is mundane and raise it to holiness. Nothing accomplishes this more than keeping kosher.

All things considered, a *Noahide Ger* is not duty-bound to observe the Jewish dietary laws, other than refraining from eating the limb of a living animal. But if he or she elects to do more than this, the observances should be taken seriously, not on and off again, eating *glatt* kosher one day and ham and cheese the next. Equally important, to be truly observant requires **observing one's observances**, remaining conscious of them and performing them with love and joy. The Hebrew word for this mindfulness is *kavana*, which means both focus and devotion. Everything depends on *kavana*. With the right *kavana*, a person could walk through a wall or fly through the air. Or eat like a human being.

✡ ✡ ✡ ✡

"Man does not live by bread alone, but by every word that comes out of the mouth of the Eternal does man live (Deuteronomy 8:3)."

The simple meaning here is that man is not alive if he is immersed in physicality alone. He must also enter the spiritual realm to be considered alive, for it is impossible to hold a gram of wisdom in a spoon.

It is not the physical bread that sustains a person in life. The word of God which is the life force of the bread is what sustains a person in life.[54]

---

54. The soul is connected to the body by virtue of food and drink. Stop eating and drinking and the soul departs.

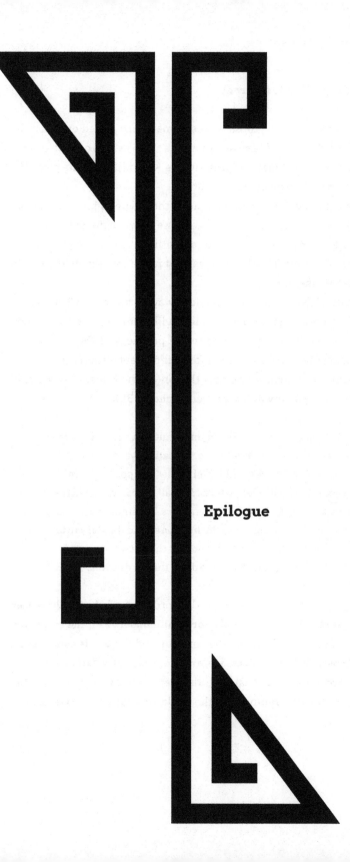

Epilogue

Ger – The Fourth Estate in Israel

At the Passover Seder, three pieces of matza are placed one atop the other on the Seder plate. These represent the three estates of the nation of Israel. The top piece of matza represents the Kohen, the middle piece the Levite, and the bottom piece the Israelite.

As the Seder begins, the middle piece, the Levite, is broken into two pieces. One piece is returned to the Seder plate between the Kohen and the Israelite. The other piece is hidden away until the end of the meal as the *afikoman*, the dessert. This broken piece of matza represents the fourth estate in Israel – the *Ger*.

The truth of the *Ger* has been hidden away for more than 2,500 years, since the destruction of the First Temple. It will be fully realized only when the Third Temple is built according to the prophecy of Ezekiel.[1] In that Temple, during the festival of Sukkot following a Sabbatical Year, all Israel will be commanded to come and hear the king of the House of David read the book of Deuteronomy, as it says (Deuteronomy 31:10-12):

> And Moses commanded them, saying, "At the end of every seven years, the set time of the Sabbatical year, during the Festival of Sukkot, when all Israel comes to appear before the Lord your God in the place which He shall choose, you shall read this Torah before all Israel in their ears. Assemble the nation, the men and the women and the little ones, and the **Ger within your gates**, that they may hear and that they may learn and fear the Lord your God and observe to do all the words of this Torah."

There, in the Holy Temple before the Lord our God, **the Noahide Ger is commanded to learn the whole Torah and observe all the mitzvoth**. There, in the Holy Temple before the Lord our God, **the Ger is established and confirmed as the fourth estate, an integral part of "all Israel"**.

Therefore, no matter what path the Ger is traveling, it leads to the Temple. And when the Temple is in the world, the world of the *Ger* will be *shalem*, complete.

---

1. The Book of Ezekiel, chapters 40-48.

Now, what about the first broken piece of matzah, the Levite, that was returned to its place on the Seder plate between the Kohen and the Israelite?

God separated the Levites from the rest of the Children of Israel so that they could minister to Him in the Temple[2] and teach the people the way of God, as it says (2 Chronicles 35:3), *"And he [King Josiah] spoke to the Levites who teach wisdom to all Israel and who are holy to the Lord."*

Those who challenge the authority of the Levite shall be thrown down, as Moses said in his blessing to the tribe of Levi, *"Bless, O Lord, his substance and accept the work of his hands; smite through the loins of them that rise up against him, and of them that hate him that they rise not again (Deuteronomy 3:11)."*

The Levites are the elite guard and inner circle of the Lord,[3] as it says (Numbers 18:20), *"I am their portion and their inheritance."*

Concerning this, the *Rambam*[4] presents us with an amazingly brilliant teaching:

> The status of Levite is not limited to one who was born a Levite. Rather, it belongs to anyone in the world whose spirit moves him to know the Lord and to set himself apart to serve and minister to Him, to walk upright as the Lord directs him, and to throw off the yoke of materialism that mankind endures. Behold, such a person is sanctified and holy of holies; the Lord will be his portion and inheritance forever and ever. He will merit ample sustenance in this world as did the *Kohanim* and the *Leviim* in times past. Concerning this, King David, an Israelite not a Levite, said, *"Hashem is my portion and my inheritance; You are my guide and destiny."*[5]

---

2. Kohanim are also from the tribe of Levi, and are sometimes called Levites in the Torah.

3. Mishneh Torah, Laws of Jubilee Year, 13:10.

4. Mishneh Torah, Laws of the Jubilee Year 13:13.

5. Psalms 16:5.

Above all, the Levite is a Levite because he places his trust in no one other than God Himself, as it says, *"Not in any man do I put trust, nor on any angel do I rely, only on the God in Heaven Who is the God of truth, whose Torah is truth and Whose prophets are true, and Who acts generously with kindness and truth. In Him do I trust and to His glorious and holy Name do I declare praises."*[6]

So now, brother *Ger* and sister *Gioret*, you have a written invitation to enter the Kingdom of God. And this is how the invitation reads: *"And I will bless them that bless you and whoever curses you will I curse; and in you shall all the families of the earth be blessed (Genesis 12:2,3)."*

✡ ✡ ✡ ✡

Endless.

---

6. Zohar II, Vayakhel 206a.

Forty Verses From the Torah
that are Pertinent to the Ger

Genesis 15:13

And He said unto Abram: Know with certainty that your offspring shall be Ger in a land that is not theirs, and shall serve them; and they shall afflict them for four hundred years

Genesis 23:4

[Abraham rose up and said] I am a Ger and a *Toshav* [resident] with you; give me a burial place as a possession with you, so that I may bury my dead from before me.

Exodus 2:22

And she bore a son, and he [Moses] called his name Gershom; for he said: "I was a Ger in a strange land."

Exodus 12:19

Seven days there shall be be no leaven found in your houses; for whosoever eats of that which is leavened, that soul shall be cut off from the congregation of Israel, whether he be a Ger or one that is born in the land.

Exodus 12:48

And when a Ger shall dwell with you, and will keep the Passover to the Lord, let all his males be circumcised, and then let him come near and keep it; and he shall be as one that is born in the land; but no uncircumcised person shall eat of it [the Passover sacrifice].

Exodus 18:3

And her two sons one of whom was named Gershom, for he [Moses] said: "I have been a Ger in a strange land."

Exodus 20:9

But the seventh day is a Sabbath unto the Lord your God, on it you shall do no manner of work, neither you, nor your son, nor your daughter nor your manservant, nor your maidservant, nor your cattle, nor your Ger that is within your gates.

Exodus 22:20

And you shall not wrong a Ger, neither shall you oppress him; for you were Gerim in the land of Egypt

Exodus 23:9

And you shall not oppress a Ger, for you know the soul of the Ger, seeing that you were Gerim in the land of Egypt.

Exodus 23:12

Six days you shall you do your work, but on the seventh day you shall rest, so that your ox and your donkey may have rest, and the son of your maidservant and the Ger may be refreshed.

Leviticus 16:29

And it [Yom Kippur] shall be for you an eternal decree: in the seventh month on the tenth day of the month, you shall afflict your souls, and shall do no manner of work, neither the native born nor the Ger who dwells among you.

Leviticus 17:8

And you shall say unto them: Any man of the House of Israel or of the Ger who dwells among them that offers a burnt-offering or sacrifice, and does not bring it to the entrance of the Tent of Meeting as to prepare it for the Lord, that man shall be cut off from his people.

Leviticus 17:10

Any man of the House of Israel or of the Ger who dwells among them who will consume any blood, I shall turn My attention to the soul who consumed the blood and I will cut him off from among his people.

Leviticus 18:26

But you shall observe My statutes and My judgments and you shall not do any of these [sexual] abominations; neither the native born nor the Ger who dwells among you.

Leviticus 19:33

When a Ger dwells with you in your land, you shall not ridicule him; do him no wrong.

Leviticus 19:34

The Ger who dwells with you shall be like a native born, and you shall love him like yourself, for you were Gerim in the land of Egypt, I am Hashem, your God.

Leviticus 20:2

Say to the Children of Israel: Any man of the Children of Israel   or of the Ger who dwells with Israel, who gives of his offspring to [the false god] Molech, shall surely be put to death; the people of the land shall stone him.

Leviticus 22:18,19

Speak to Aaron and to his sons and to all the Children of Israel, and say to them: Any man of the House of Israel or of the Gerim among Israel who will bring his offering to fulfill any of their vows or any of their freewill offerings, and brings it to the Lord as a burnt offering, in order for it to be favorably accepted, it must be an unblemished male from the herd or from the flock of sheep or goats.

Leviticus 24:16

Whoever blasphemes the Name of Hashem shall surely be put to death, all the congregation shall stone him; whether a Ger or a native born, if he blasphemes the Name, he shall be put to death.

Leviticus 25:23

The land shall not be sold in perpetuity, for the land is Mine and you are Gerim and residents with Me.

Leviticus 25:47, 48

And if a Ger who dwells alongside you grows rich, and your brother grows poor beside him, and is sold to the Ger Toshav with you or to the descendant of the Ger's family; after he is sold he may be redeemed; one of his brothers may redeem him.

Numbers 9:14

And if a Ger shall dwell with you, and will make a Passover offering to Hashem, according to the law of the Passover offering and its decree so shall he do; one law shall be for you – for the Ger and for one who was born in the land.

Numbers 15:14

And if a Ger dwells with you or one who is among you throughout your generations, and will bring a fire-offering, a sweet savour unto Hashem, just as you do, so shall he do.

Numbers 15:15

For the congregation – the same law shall be for you and for the Ger who dwells, an eternal decree for you and for the Ger who dwells with you.

Numbers 15:16

One law and one decree will be for you and for the Ger who dwells with you.

Numbers 19:10

And the one who gathered the ashes of the [red] cow shall immerse his clothes, and he will be unclean until evening; and it shall be an eternal law for the Children of Israel and for the Ger who dwells among them.

Numbers 35:15

For the Children of Israel and for the Ger and for the settler among them, shall these six cities be a refuge, so that anyone who kills a person unintentionally may flee there.

Deuteronomy 5:13,14

Six days shall you labor and do all you work; but the seventh day is a Sabbath to the Lord your God, on it you shall do no manner of work, you and your son and your daughter and your manservant and your maidservant and your ox and your donkey and all your animals and the Ger who is within your gates, so that your manservant and your maidservant may rest like you.

Deuteronomy 10:18

He carries out justice for the fatherless and widow, and loves the Ger in giving him food and clothing.

Deuteronomy 14:21

You shall not eat of anything that dies of itself; you may give it to the Ger who is within your gates that he may eat it; or you may sell it to a *Nochri* (foreigner); for you are a holy people to the Lord your God; you shall not boil a kid in its mother's milk.

Deuteronomy 23:8

You shall not hate an Edomite because he is your brother; you shall not hate an Egyptian because you were a Ger in his land.

Deuteronomy 24:14

You shall not oppress a hired servant that is poor and needy, whether he be of your brothers or of your Ger who are in your land within your gates.

Deuteronomy 24:17

You shall not pervert the justice due the Ger or the orphan, nor shall you take the clothing of a widow as a pledge.

Deuteronomy 26:11

And you shall rejoice over all the good which the Lord your God has given to you, and to your house, you, and the Levite, and the Ger that is in the midst of you.

Deuteronomy 26:12

When you have completed tithing all the tithe of your produce in the third year, the year of tithing, you shall give it to the Levite to the Ger, to the orphan, and to the widow, that they may eat it within your gates and be satisfied.

Deuteronomy 27:19

Cursed be one who perverts the justice due the Ger, the fatherless, and the widow. And all the people shall say, "Amen."

Deuteronomy 28:43

The Ger that is among you shall ascend above you higher and higher; and you shall descend lower and lower. He will lend to you, but you will not lend to him; he will be a head and you will be a tail.

Deuteronomy 29:9,10

You are all standing here today, all of you, before Hashem your God – your tribal heads, your elders and your officers, all the men of Israel. Your little ones, your wives, and your Ger that is in the midst of your camp, from the hewer of your wood to the drawer of your water.

Deuteronomy 31:12

Assemble the people, the men and the women, and the little ones, and your Ger that is within your gates, so that they may hear, and that they may learn, and fear the Lord your God, and be careful to perform all the words of this Torah.

Isaiah 14:1

For the Lord will have mercy on Jacob, and will again choose Israel, and place them in their land, and the Ger shall accompany them, and they shall be added onto the House of Jacob.

acum	idolater
aggadot	Torah stories and parables
Ain Techila	without beginning
aiver min hachai	limb of a living animal
aravot	willow branches; the seventh heaven
aron	box; the Holy Ark
Ashkenazim	German or eastern European Jews
Assiah	World of Action
Atzilut	World of Emanation
avatar	manifestation of a deity; associated with idolatry
avodah zarah	idolatry; strange worship
b'ezrat Hashem	with the help of God
B'nai Noah	Children of Noah
B'nai Yisrael	Children of Israel
B'nei Neviim	School of Prophets in days of Elijah and Elisha
batei dinim	rabbinic courts of law

ben necher	stranger; non-Jew (identical with nochri)
berachot	blessings
Beta Yisrael	black Ethiopian Jews
Beth Rimmon	Aramean idol
Briah	World of Creation; World of Throne of Glory
brit	covenant
brit milah	covenant of circumcision
capporet	atonement; golden cover of Holy Ark
chametz	leavened bread; foodstuffs with leavening
chayot	category of angels
chelev	certain forbidden animal fats
chen	grace; mercy
cherubim	category of angels; golden angels atop Holy Ark
Chumash	Five books of Moses
davar	word; thing
El	God; Name of God associated with power and kindness

erev Shabbat	day before Sabbath
eshel	tamarisk tree
etrog	citron; one of four types of plants waved on Sukkot
Etz HaDaat	Tree of Knowledge
ezrach	native born Jew
Gan Eden	Garden of Eden
Gehinnom	Purgatory
gematria	numerical value Hebrew words
Ger b'Shaarecha	Noahide living among Jews
Ger Toshav	Noahide living in Israel
Ger Tzedek	Jewish convert; saintly Gentile
Gerim	plural of Jewish converts or righteous Noahides
geulah	redemption
gilui Shechina	Revelation of God
Gioret	Female convert or saintly female Noahide
glatt	smooth; high level of kosher meat

gulgalta	skull; term used for Keter (Crown) in Kabbalah
hadassim	myrtle branches (sing. hadas)
Haggadah	book read at the Passover Seder
halacha	Jewish law as per rabbinic tradition
halak	smooth; high level of kosher (same as glatt)
Hasid	pious person; follower of Baal Shem Tov
Hasidei Umot HaOlam	Pious Gentiles
havdalah	ceremony at conclusion of Shabbat
hechsher	rabbinic certification
Kabbalah	esoteric teachings of Torah
Kabbalist	Master of Kabbalah
kashrut	status of food according to halacha
kavana	intention; focus
kavod	honor; glory
kedusha	holiness
kelipot	unclean spiritual husks

Kenites	descendants of Jethro
Keter	highest Divine Emanation
ketoret	Holy Temple incense
kiddush	sanctification of Sabbath over cup of wine
kishuf	magic or witchcraft
Kohanim	Jewish priests
Kohen	Jewish priest
kosher	fitting, permissible
kasher	to make something kosher
kugel	quiche or pudding, usually noodles or potatoes
lechem mishneh	two loaves of bread at Shabbat meals
livuy	accompaniment
lulav	palm frond; one of four types of plants on Sukkot
m'gaier	conversion as a Jew
m'gaieret	fem. of m'gaier
Malchut	Kingdom; the tenth Divine Emanation

manna	heavenly food eaten by Israel in the Wilderness
Mashiach	Messiah
matzah	unleavened bread
mazal	destiny; spiritual path
melacha	work; forbidden work on Shabbat
Menorah	seven branch candelabra in Holy Temple
mesirat nefesh	self-sacrifice
Messianic Era	Era of Final Redemption
Metatron	name of angelic prince
midrash	metaphorical teachings of Torah
mikra	accident; mere happening
mikvah	ritual immersion pool
Mishnah	primary codification of Oral Tradition
mitzvah	commandment; good deed; pl. mitzvot
mizbeyach	sacrificial altar
moror	bitter herbs (eaten at Passover Seder)

muchshar	meat that has been made kosher by removing the blood.
nachas	satisfaction, pleasure, feeling of pride
nachash	serpent
nachem	comfort
nafash	refreshed
Nasi Elohim	Prince of God
Nazirite	person who vows to abstain from wine, etc.
nefesh	person; lowest aspect of soul
neshama	high aspect of the soul (relates to intellect)
nevelah	animal that died other than by kosher slaughter
nigleh	revealed parts of Torah (Scripture, Jewish Law, etc.)
nikkur	removing the sciatic nerve (gid hanasha)
nistor	esoteric parts of Torah (Kabbalah, Chassidut)
Noahide	Gentile who observes the Seven Universal Laws
Noahide Ger	Gentile who observes the Seven Universal Laws and takes on additional Torah observances

Nochri	Gentile who has not taken on the Seven Universal Laws
ochel	food
Ohr HaGanuz	hidden light of God
omer	measurement of dry food (2.114 liters)
oneg Shabbat	pleasurable Shabbat experience (mostly from food)
Oral Tradition	explanations of Written Torah.
parve	neither meat nor milk
Paschal lamb	Passover sacrifice eaten Seder night.
Raphael	an archangel, primarily associated with healing
ratzah	desire; to accept favorably
Rosh Hashanah	first day of the new Jewish year
Ruach Elohim	the spirit of God
ruach hakodesh	the holy spirit; low level of prophecy
sarim	ministers, referring to people or angels
se'or	sour dough used as a leavening agent
Sefardic Jews	Jews from Spain; oriental Jews

Sefer Raziel	book given by angel to Adam, the first man.
Sephirot	Divine Emanations by which God directs the world
Seraphim	angels associated with the Throne of Glory
Shabbat	day upon which God rested from creation; seventh day of the week; Saturday
Shaddai	Name of God
shamor	observe; protect; Sabbath observance
Shechina	revealed Presence of God
shechita	kosher slaughter of animals for food
shina	sleep
shochet	Jewish ritual slaughterer
shofar	ram's horn
Shulchan Arukh	Code of Jewish Law
siddur	prayer book
Sivan	Third month of the year; month in which Torah given on Mount Sinai
Sukkot	Jewish holiday celebrating ingathering of crops; temporary dwellings during holiday of Sukkot

Sulam	ladder; appellation of prominent Kabbalist
tachash	animal whose skins were on roof of Tabernacle
tahara	purification; purity
tahor	pure; innocent
Talmud Torah	study of Torah; Jewish day school
teva	nature (with letter Tet); Noah's Ark (with letter Tav)
tikun	rectification; perfected
tohu	chaos
Torah	God's Law, instructions
traifah	lit. torn; forbidden food
trayber	Yiddish term for removal of sciatic nerve
tzadik	righteous person; saint
tzadik yesod olam	righteous person as foundation of the world
tzedaka	righteousness; charity
tzitzith	knotted strings on four corners of garment as per the Torah
Yah	Name of God

yeshiva	school of Torah learning
yetzer hara	evil inclination of man
Yetzirah	formation; the world of angels
YHVH	Four-Letter Name of God
Yom Kippur	Day of Atonement
zachor	remembrance; Sabbath observance
zaraath	spiritual leprosy mandated by Torah
zer	crown
Zion	place that marks Presence of God; Holy Temple, Jerusalem, Israel
Zohar	Kabbalistic commentary on the Torah, ascribed to Rebbe Shimon bar Yochai and his colleagues
zuhama	spiritual filth that entered soul of man after the sin of the Tree of Knowledge, and again after sin of the Golden Calf
z"l	may he (or she) be remembered for a blessing
zy"a	may his (or her) merit protect us

Made in the USA
Middletown, DE
08 January 2020